RANGERS

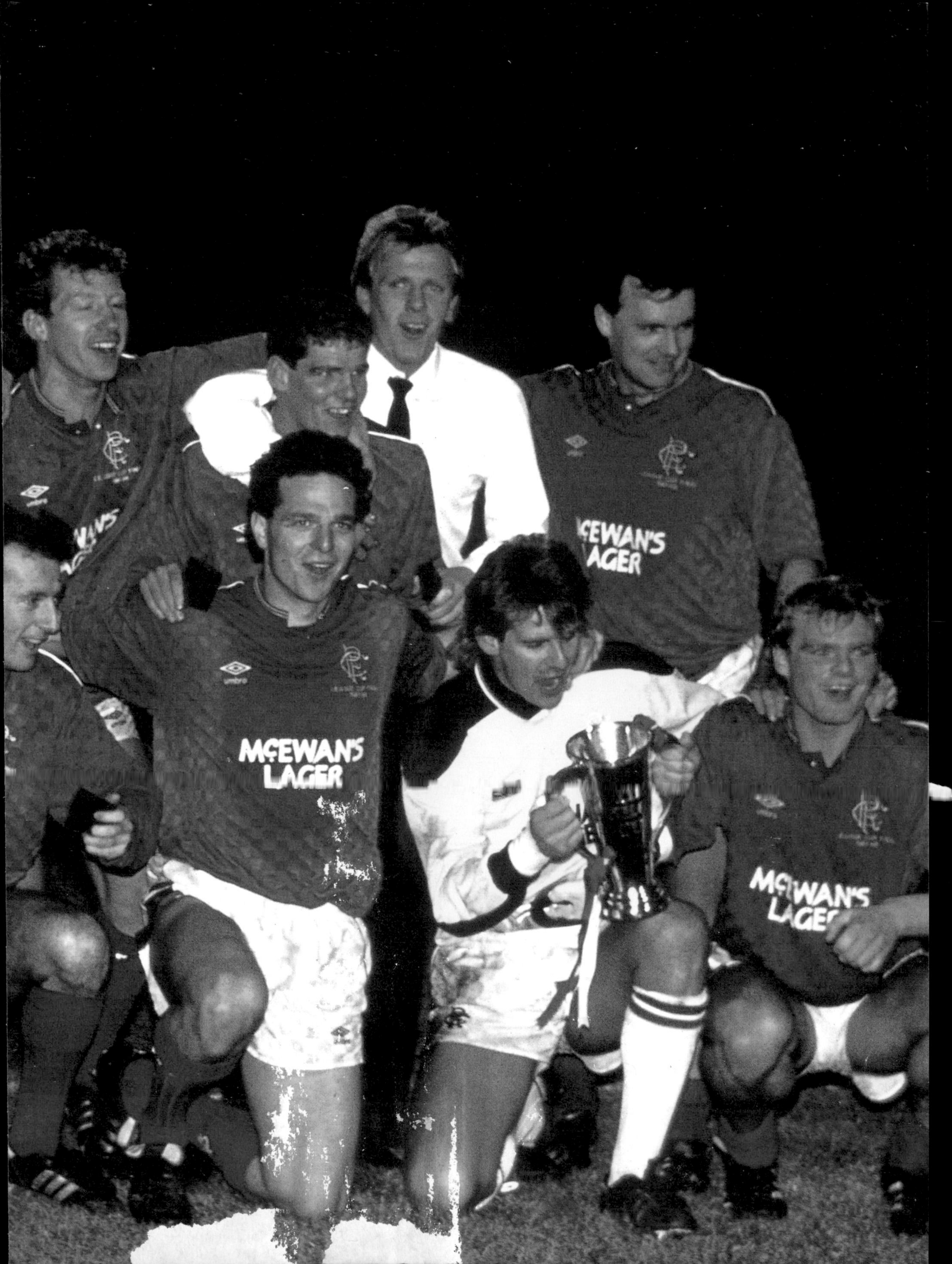
McEWAN'S LAGER
McEWAN'S LAGER
McEWAN'S LAGER

RANGERS

Ian Morrison

HAMLYN

Player-Manager Graeme Souness at his desk at Ibrox.

Cover picture *Graeme Souness in action.*

Endpapers *Rangers squad celebrate victory over Aberdeen in the Skol Cup final, October 1987.*

Title spread *Davie Cooper (11) blasts Rangers' first goal past keeper Jim Leighton in the 1987 Skol Cup final.*

Pages 10–11 *Rangers immortal Jim Baxter (left) tangles with Dundee United's Scott in an August 1969 league match.*

Contents

Published in 1988 by
The Hamlyn Publishing Group Limited,
a division of The Octopus Publishing Group,
Michelin House, 81 Fulham Road, London SW3 6RB,
and distributed for them by
Octopus Distribution Services Limited,
Rushden, Northamptonshire NN10 9RZ

© 1988 The Hamlyn Publishing Group Limited

ISBN 0 600 558 86X

Printed in Spain

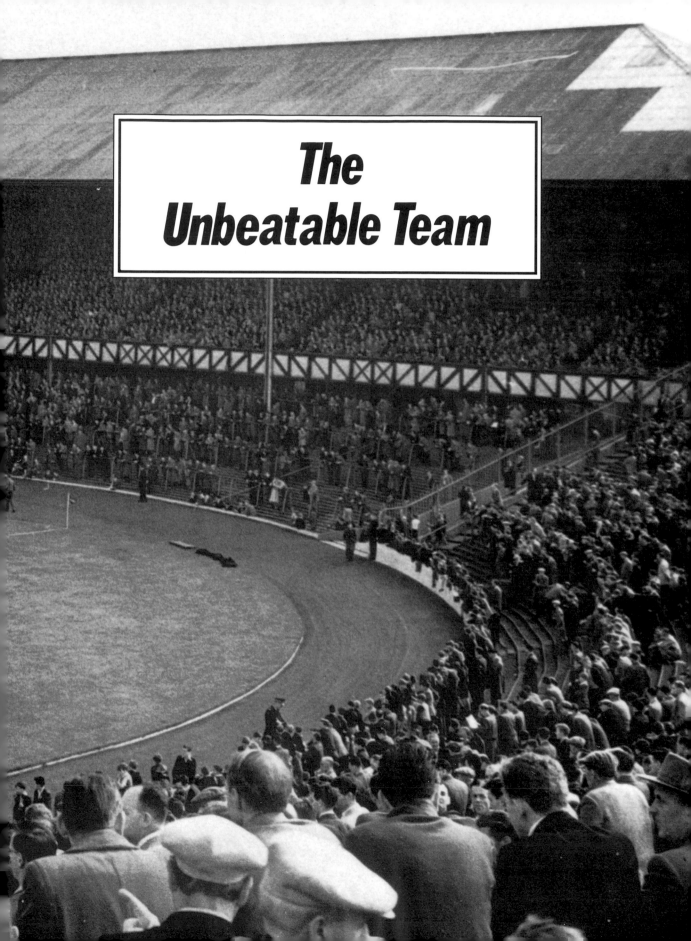

The Unbeatable Team

Pages 12–13 *Ibrox stadium in
the 1940s.*

Pages 14–15 *Skipper John Greig
tours a packed Ibrox in a pony
and trap on Gala Day 1975.*

The trophy room at Ibrox Stadium has been adorned with more silverware than that of any other club in Britain. But for a club that started from such humble beginnings, its rise to greatness is an achievement in itself.

It all started in the spring of 1872, the year before the formation of the Scottish Football Association. Queen Victoria was little more than half-way through her reign and the likes of the motor-car and European football competitions were things of the future.

The motor car and European football are now part of every day life. So too are Glasgow Rangers, one of the biggest names in world soccer.

The club was founded by a group of young men, mostly from the Gareloch, who were in search of a leisurely pursuit other than rowing on the Clyde. The three youngsters, all from Protestant families, were Peter Campbell, Tom Vallance and Moses McNeil. They brought their boat ashore at Fleshers' Haugh on Glasgow Green in the East End. There they saw a group of lads playing football. The team they admired were the Eastern FC, who had been formed a few months earlier. The three youngsters were impressed and decided to form a team of their own. McNeil had six brothers and it was hoped they would help with making up the numbers. But only three of them, William, Peter and Harry, were keen on taking up this new pastime.

They eventually mustered enough support and in May 1872 played their first match on Eastern's pitch. For many years historians incorrectly dated the club's birth as 1873 and, in fact, the club celebrated its centenary in 1973. But documentary evidence shows the club was founded one year earlier. Their first game was under the name of Argyle and their opponents were a team styled as Clyde. The McNeils were the backbone of those early teams and it was Moses McNeil who suggested the name Rangers after he spotted it in C.W. Alcock's *English Football Manual*. The Rangers was the name of an English Rugby club at the time (it's a good job Harlequins or Rosslyn Park didn't attract Moses' attention instead!).

The club's Protestant support stems back to the days of Campbell, Vallance and McNeil, who all happened to be non-Catholics. But a theory that religion became the overriding factor in distinguishing between Rangers and Celtic dates to the First World War, when Belfast shipbuilders Harland and Wolff opened a yard in Glasgow. Most of the staff were Irishmen, and Orangemen at that, and they attached themselves to Rangers because of Celtic's traditional Irish Catholic connections.

After their opening friendly, Rangers arranged more matches at Fleshers' Haugh against Eastern, Callander, Star of Leven and Rovers. But the strongest and oldest (1867) team of the day, Queen's Park, refused to play them, using the excuse that they did not have their own ground. But the McNeil brothers had ambitions. The club joined the Scottish Football Association and, in October 1874, Rangers lined up for their first Scottish Cup tie, against Oxford. The game was played at the Queen's Park Recreation Ground and Rangers won 2-0; but Dumbarton put paid to any further ambitions by winning 1-0 afer a replay in the next round.

In 1875 Rangers found a ground of their own at Burnbank in the West End of the city. Because they had their own ground it meant Queen's Park could no longer shun their request to play them in a friendly. Before meeting Queen's Park, Rangers had held Vale of Leven and Clydesdale to draws at Glasgow Green. But they wanted to test their skills against the might of Scotland's top team.

Rangers were only too pleased to go to Hampden for the first match between the two clubs. Although Queen's Park won 2-0, the men in blue did themselves proud that day.

QUEEN'S PARK FOOTBALL CLUB
SEASON 1873-74.

It was during their time at Burnbank that one of the greatest goalkeepers in the club's history joined Rangers. George Gillespie came as either a full-back or wing-half, but he was to be badly hurt in the third game against Vale of Leven in the 1877 Cup Final. He was out of the game for a while and when he returned it was as goalkeeper. Coincidentally, two of his immediate successors, Jim McAuley and Harry Rennie, both started life as outfielders.

After only one season at Burnbank, Rangers moved to a new ground at Kinning Park. They stayed there for the next 11 seasons. The new ground had a clubhouse and grandstand which the previous tenants, Clydesdale, had erected. The playing surface was regarded as one of the finest in Scotland. The foundations had been laid for the birth of a great club. But they still had to play second fiddle to Queen's Park, Renton, Clydesdale and Vale of Leven.

Within four years of their formation Rangers appeared in their first Scottish Cup final. They were up against the crack Vale of Leven side who, in the fifth round in 1877, had become the first Scottish side to beat Queen's Park. They were odds-on favourites to win the trophy and when the two teams came out on to the pitch it was obvious it was a 'men' versus 'boys' clash. But the youngsters from Rangers shocked Vale by holding them to a goalless draw at Hamilton Crescent.

In the replay Rangers were desperately unlucky not to win. At the end of 90 minutes it was 1-1 and the tie went into extra time. Towards the end of the

The aristocrats of early Scottish football, Queen's Park have retained their amateur status to this day. Seen here is their 1873–4 side, winners of the first Scottish FA Cup final.

VALE OF LEVEN FOOTBALL TEAM

extra period one of their forwards, Peter Campbell, collected the ball, beat two men and shot past the Vale 'keeper. In those days there were no goal nets, or even crossbars, and the crowd was packed close behind the Vale goal. The ball hit one of the fans, who was standing a good foot behind the line. To the Rangers' disbelief, the Vale keeper was next seen gathering the ball and kicking it upfield. Play continued despite the Rangers' protests to the referee.

The club lodged a complaint to the Scottish FA and the fan whom the ball hit, a notable surgeon of the day, Sir George B. MacLeod, was prepared to give evidence under oath that the ball was behind the line. But the SFA would not accept his testimony and ordered a third match, which Vale of Leven won 3-2 at Hampden. In defeat however, the Glasgow men showed maturity which belied their inexperience. Suddenly, they had shown the football world they could not be treated lightly.

Two years later, in 1879, Rangers appeared in their second final. Again it was against Vale of Leven. Struthers opened the scoring for Rangers, who dominated the game, and a second Struthers strike seemed to have the trophy sewn up. But the referee disallowed what looked a perfectly good goal because of an offside infringement. Vale of Leven equalised near the end and Rangers were deprived of their first Scottish Cup win.

Another protest was lodged, and again the SFA ordered a replay. But this time Rangers were not prepared to be told what to do when they knew they were right. In protest they did not turn up for the second game.

After the second Cup Final defeat there was a decline in Rangers' fortunes and enthusiasm waned. A financial crisis loomed and in 1879 it was felt a change of strip would reverse their luck. They tried playing in blue and white hooped shirts, but reverted to their royal blue in 1883, the year Willie Wilton joined the club. A key to Rangers' success over the years has been in appointing the right man for the right job. And Willie Wilton was the first of their great managers.

Originally secretary to the reserve team, he became secretary/manager when the club became a limited liability company in 1899. His influence over the club for more than 30 years was immense. A man of tremendous vision, he insisted upon the grandstand being built at Ibrox because he foresaw the growth in soccer. He also organised the running track around the pitch because he wanted athletics at Ibrox as well as football. And he was also instrumental in insisting Rangers players dressed immaculately on and off the field. This is a tradition that has been maintained over the years. It was Wilton who changed the Rangers colours back to their traditional royal blue after the experiment with blue and white hoops.

Over the years the Scottish FA Cup has seen many unusual incidents and protests but in November 1884 Rangers were involved in one of the strangest. After losing 4-3 at Arbroath, Rangers protested that the pitch was not wide enough. It was measured at 49 yards 1 inch . . . 11 inches short of the 50-yard minimum. The game was replayed five weeks later and Rangers won 8-1! In 1885 the club defected from the Scottish FA and affiliated to the English Football Association. It was about this time that Rangers had been losing some of their top players to English clubs, who had adopted professionalism. Rangers' attitude was, 'if you can't beat them, join them'. In 1887, during their spell 'south of the border', they had the distinction of emulating Queen's Park and reached the semi-final of the English Cup. They lost to the eventual winners, Aston Villa, 3-1.

They returned 'home' later that year and, after Wilton's search for a better ground, they moved to their new home at Ibrox, which was opened on 20 August with the great Preston North End side as the first visitors. Not on the same site as the present-day stadium, it was, nevertheless, not too far away, near Copland Road. The following year arch rivals Celtic were formed. Rangers were now 15 years old, but pedigree counted for nothing in Celtic's eyes as they started their first official match.

Rangers' reputation did not overawe the newcomers and the home team won the first of many encounters between the two giants of Scottish football. The game was billed as a friendly but such a billing does not exist in Rangers–Celtic matches. So, the 'Greatest Club Match in the World' was born. Only 2,000 spectators witnessed it.

When the Scottish League was formed in 1890 it gave Rangers a chance to

Rangers' 1896–7 side, which hammered Dumbarton 5-1 in the Scottish Cup final at Hampden.

show their real worth in a season-long competition against the best of the Scottish teams, which now included Celtic. Rangers proved they had the stamina to negotiate such a tournament successfully and emerged as joint champions with Dumbarton after a play-off. That title was to be the first of many for Rangers. On 21 March 1891 Rangers and Celtic lined up in the first of their League meetings, at Parkhead. Goals by Kerr and McCreadie helped secure a 2-2 draw. Celtic won the return match at Ibrox and the following year the men from Parkhead won their first trophy when they took the Cup. And so began the Glasgow domination of Scottish football which has gone on for nearly 100 years.

Rangers finished second to Celtic in the League in 1893, but gained revenge by winning the first of more than 30 Glasgow Cup finals 3-1 at Cathkin Park. Professionalism had been adopted in Scotland in 1893 and the following year Rangers lifted the Scottish Cup for the first time when they beat Celtic 3-1 in front of 17,000 at Hampden.

Between then and the turn of the century the Blues won the Cup twice, in 1897 and 1898, beating Dumbarton 5-1 and Kilmarnock 2-0. The win over Kilmarnock heralded the start of one of the most remarkable runs in Scottish football. They won all 18 games in the League in 1898–9, and won four cup ties, all without a replay. Their run of consecutive wins stood at 23 when they played Celtic in the Cup Final at Hampden – but the Parkhead men put an end to their winning streak with a 2-0 victory. Rangers won the League that season by 10 points from Hearts and scored 79 goals in 18 matches, conceding a mere 18. They emulated the feat of Celtic, who had also gone unbeaten the previous season. To this day these are the only two instances of First/Premier Division teams going through a season unbeaten.

That great championship season of 1898–99 started a run of four successive titles, and to make it even sweeter, Celtic were runners-up on three occasions.

Ibrox was re-built in 1899 and at the turn of the century it was hailed as one of the finest grounds in Britain. One of its notable features was the wooden grandstand and pavilion; the terracing was also of wooden construction. But on 5 April 1902 Ibrox was the scene of one of the worst disasters in British football.

It happened during a Scotland versus England international with 60,000 fans packed in the ground. One of the Scottish heroes that day was outside left Bobby Templeton. A bit of a dandy in his day, Templeton had the ball skills of Stanley Matthews. Every time he got the ball the crowd expected the unusual and as he made a run towards one of the corner flags, every neck wrenched to get a view of him. As the crowd surged forward, the wooden terracing gave way and a gaping hole appeared into which fell hundreds of screaming, panicking fans. The casualty list read 25 dead and 500 injured.

Remarkably, the game went on, with the officials, players and spectators on the opposite side of the ground unaware of the disaster. From that day wooden terraces were banned at football grounds. (Sadly, a similar tragedy was to occur 69 years later, with even more serious consequences.)

Earlier that season Celtic generated a bit of ill-feeling between the two Glasgow giants. Rangers had been presented with a trophy called the Glasgow Exhibition Cup as a result of winning a tournament which was one

Davie Meiklejohn leads the side out at Ibrox in the late 1920s. Captain of both Rangers and Scotland, he was a commanding figure in the defence. He played 635 games for the Light Blues, winning 11 championship and four Cup-winner's medals.

Rangers' all-conquering 1929–30 side won the championship (for the fourth year in succession) and beat Partick Thistle in the Cup final after a replay.

of the attractions of the Glasgow International Exhibition at Kelvingrove Park. The club decided to re-name the trophy the British League Cup to be contested by the top two teams in England and the top two in Scotland. Sunderland and Everton were the English representatives while, naturally, Rangers and Celtic represented Scotland. Rangers defeated Everton and Celtic beat Sunderland, so the 'Auld Firm' met in the final. After extra time Celtic won 3-2. That's when the trouble started.

When the Exhibition authorities first presented the Cup, the Scottish League Committee were asked if they would run the tournament. Celtic put forward a motion that the Cup should become the property of the club winning it with the *option* of presenting it to the League for an annual competition. But, after winning it, Celtic kept the trophy and it was never played for again.

After beating Hearts to win the Scottish Cup at Celtic Park in 1903, Rangers had to endure seven seasons without bringing a major 'pot' to Ibrox. There was a chance to get some silverware back into the Ibrox trophy cabinet in 1909 when they reached the Cup Final. After drawing 2-2 with Celtic in front of 70,000 fervent fans at Hampden, the two teams also drew the replay, this time 1-1. Confusion arose about the playing of extra time. Suddenly a riot broke out. Both sets of fans ripped wood from the stands and started bonfires. They also set fire to the pay boxes. The emergency services could not get near the ground. The scenes were ugly and disgraceful. The Scottish FA suggested a third match at a venue away from Glasgow, but the two clubs thought it better not to play at all. Consequently the Cup was withheld and no medals were awarded.

But Rangers did not have to wait much longer to get their hands on a trophy again. They won the League in 1911 by four points from Aberdeen. That success heralded the start of one of the finest eras in the club's history. With players such as Jimmy Gordon, Alec Smith, Alec Bennett, Jimmy Bowie, Willie Reid and Jimmy Galt, they left Celtic in their wake as they completed a hat-trick of League triumphs in 1911–13. But then it was Celtic who chalked up four successive championships. Rangers ended their run in 1918 when they won the championship by a solitary point. Celtic regained the upper hand in 1919 but the following season 106 goals in 42 matches was enough for Rangers to win their tenth title. Rangers lost only two of the 42 League games – to Motherwell in their ninth game and to Clydebank in game number 34. In Andy Cunningham, who joined the club from Kilmarnock in 1915, Rangers had discovered a prolific striker. He went on to score 201 goals in 447 games for Rangers and was capped 22 times by Scotland.

Despite being the runaway winners of the League in 1920, the Cup jinx still haunted Rangers: they had not taken the trophy since 1903. They lost at the semi-final stage after three games against Albion Rovers, who were destined to finish bottom of the League that season. Then, on 2 May 1920, tragedy struck. Willie Wilton was killed in a drowning accident at Gourock. This was more than just a personal loss: Wilton had put Rangers on the road to prosperity and success, as Ibrox crowds soared to the 80,000 mark. Could such a great man ever be replaced?

Trainer Bill Struth was invited to take charge of the team. He stayed 34 years. The appointment of Wilton had been a great move by the club. The appointment of Struth was another master stroke. If Wilton was the man who turned Rangers from an ordinary football club into a great one, then Struth was the man who turned them into the giants they are today.

Struth was a stonemason and a professional runner. He knew very little about football, but was one of the best when it came to fitness and discipline. His methods were to create a Rangers side which completely overshadowed

Alan Morton joined Rangers from Queen's Park in 1920 (he was Bill Struth's first and most inspired signing) and was the outstanding member of the team for the next dozen years. On his retirement in 1932 he went straight onto the Rangers' board.

all opposition. He had been the trainer at Clyde when Rangers recruited him towards the end of the 1913–14 season, following the death of Jimmy Wilson. A forceful character, Struth had the knack of turning ordinary players into great players.

'I know you can play, laddie; but can you play for *us*?' he would often ask. It was to become his legendary catchphrase.

In his first full season in charge, 1920–21, Struth guided the club to a 10-point margin over Celtic in the Scottish League. Their 76 points out of a possible 84 was a British record, and they won 35 of 42 games, losing only once (0-2 at home to Celtic). Andy Cunningham knocked in 29 league and cup goals as attendances soared: the four games against Celtic that season drew crowds of nearly 300,000. But, despite those records, that elusive double would not come their way; Partick Thistle saw to that with a 1-0 win at Celtic Park in the 1921 Cup final.

The backbone of Struth's team – and Scotland's, for that matter – was skipper Davie Meiklejohn. A giant of a man, he was powerfully built and completely authoritative on the field. He joined Rangers in 1919 and served them loyally for 19 years. To complement the abundant wealth of talent waiting to be nurtured, Struth got the cheque book out and made Queen's Park winger Alan Morton his first signing.

Only 5ft 4in, Morton was immensely quick, with magnificent close control and pinpoint-accurate centres. He was the scourge of opposing defences and an idol of millions of Scots, not just Rangers fans. In all he played 495 games for Rangers and scored 115 goals. One of Morton's greatest matches was in 1928, but this time it was wearing the blue of Scotland, not Rangers. He was a member of the 'Wembley Wizards' who destroyed England 5-1. It was his crosses that enabled outside right Alex Jackson to score a hat-trick, and earned him the soubriquet 'Wee Blue Devil'. After retiring he maintained his connections with Rangers when he joined the board of directors.

Even Morton's magic could not conjure up another championship success in 1921–2, when Rangers came agonisingly close to both league and cup titles: they had to be content with the runners-up spot in both competitions, to Celtic and Morton respectively. They lost the league by one point and, had Morton, Meiklejohn and Sandy Archibald not been on international duty when Rangers played (and lost 0-2) at Motherwell, it could well have been a hat-trick of championships.

But Struth had built a team capable of overcoming such reverses and he guided them to three consecutive league triumphs in 1923–25. On each occasion Airdrieonians, inspired by the great Hughie Gallacher, finished runners-up.

For a club that had emerged as virtually invincible it was hard to comprehend how the Light Blues should slip to sixth place in the league in 1925–26, their worst ever finish even to this day. But if you look closer you will see they were struck by some cruel luck from the start of the season, notably with injuries. Skipper Meiklejohn played only 12 games during the campaign. For a man who averaged nearly 40 games per season over 17 years it is clear to see how his absence affected the team.

That temporary setback was enough to spur Rangers on to even greater glories. The next season they headed the league for the 15th time. It started a run of five successive titles; moreover, in the 13 seasons between 1926 and the outbreak of the Second World War in 1939, they won the title no fewer than 10 times, finished runner-up twice (behind the wonderful Motherwell side in 1932, and Celtic in 1936) and were third in 1938.

Bob McPhail joined the club from Airdrie in 1927 and took over the inside

'Big Jimmy' Smith, a great favourite with Ibrox fans, was signed from East Sterling. A prolific striker, he scored over 300 goals in his career, topping the Scottish League list in 1933–4 with 41 goals.

forward role from Tommy Cairns. In his 12 years at Ibrox, McPhail scored 233 goals – a club record that still stands. He also won six Scottish Cup-winners' medals with Rangers. He had already won one with Airdrie (alongside Hughie Gallacher) in 1924 when they enjoyed the greatest moment in their history. McPhail soon fitted into the strong Rangers team and his partnership with Alan Morton was to help steer the club to five championships before Morton's retirement in 1932–3.

Morton's skills and McPhail's goalscoring talents turned 1927–8 into one of the club's greatest seasons. They saw Celtic finish five points behind them in the league and then, at last, they completed that much-sought-after double when they beat the Parkhead men 4-0 in front of 118,115 fans at Hampden in a match that had 18 internationals on display. The Cup had not been to Ibrox for 25 years and its absence had begun to become something of a music-hall joke – after all, Celtic had triumphed nine times in that period. When Rangers were awarded a penalty just after half-time, with the score goalless, it called for a man of skipper Meiklejohn's stature to compose himself enough to step up and put home the kick. That was the start of the second-half flood of goals. McPhail added a second before Sandy Archibald netted the last two. At last, the Cup was back at Ibrox.

Once they had got that 'double' feeling they wanted more. The league title came easily the following season but Kilmarnock were the spoilers in the cup. Killie won 2-0 – though if Rangers' Craig had converted a disputed first-half penalty it might have been a second consecutive double.

In 1929–30 nobody could stand in their way as they headed the league five points ahead of Motherwell, who were becoming quite a force at the time. In the Cup final they were taken to a replay by plucky Partick Thistle

Sam English's 44 goals for Rangers in 1931–2 remain the club's highest-ever tally for League goals in a season. English was involved in the fatal accident to Celtic and Scotland goalkeeper John Thomson in September 1931. Thomson, diving for the ball at English's feet, struck his head against the forward's knee and fractured his skull. Although blameless, English was later forced into retirement as a result of a sustained campaign of vilification by football crowds all over Scotland.

and won 2-1 after a goalless draw. Thistle, made up entirely of locally produced players, made the mighty Rangers fight all the way.

The cup bogy had now been well and truly laid. In addition to completing the double that season, Rangers had a clean sweep and won everything they entered: Glasgow Cup, Glasgow Charity Cup, Scottish Second Eleven Cup and Alliance Championship. It was the most complete domination ever seen in British football.

As men like Meiklejohn and Morton reached the end of their careers, Struth had to assemble a new team. In came the likes of Jerry Dawson, one of the finest goalkeepers to play for the club; Torry Gillick, a great joker and firm favourite with the Ibrox fans; and his fellow forward Alec Venters, who came from Cowdenbeath. But one of the biggest influences on the 'new' team was centre-forward Jimmy Smith. Signed from East Stirling after scoring 16 goals in 12 matches, he continued the goalscoring habit at Ibrox and finished up with more than 300 goals during his career.

Despite scoring 118 goals in 38 matches in 1931–2, Rangers could only finish second in the league to Motherwell, for whom Willie Macfadyen alone scored 52 out of 119! Had they clinched the title that year, Rangers would have emulated Celtic's record of six successive titles in 1905–10. Rangers' hero that season was leading scorer Sam English who netted 44 times to create the club record. But, despite losing out in the league, cup glory came to Ibrox, when they beat Kilmarnock 3-0 after a 1-1 draw.

League success returned in 1933 when they pushed Motherwell into second place as the Light Blues won their 20th championship. But the season was the last for Alan Morton. One of the greatest names in Rangers' history bowed out after more than 500 games for Queen's Park and Rangers.

Motherwell were 'bridesmaids' again to Struth's team in 1934 (when the Light Blues again notched 118 goals) and St Mirren could not prevent a third double. On their way to cup glory the 'Gers disposed of Blairgowrie 14-2 in the first round to establish a club record victory. That win was the start of an amazing Scottish Cup run in which Rangers won 20 consecutive matches. However, the final against the Buddies that season was one of the poorest ever seen at Hampden. Rangers won 5-0, but a large proportion of the 90,000 crowd had left the ground long before the final whistle. Celtic returned as a threat but Rangers won league title number 22 in 1934-5 and for the second consecutive season completed the double, this time at the expense of plucky Hamilton. The Glasgow battle swung, temporarily, to Celtic in 1935-6 as they won their first title for 10 years. Even Rangers' 110 goals were not good enough to win them a fourth successive title. But a McPhail goal in the Cup Final brought the trophy back to Ibrox for the third successive year. The opposition at Hampden was middle-of-the-table Third Lanark who put up a brave performance. It took one of Jerry Dawson's finest displays to save the day for the Ibrox men. Not since Queen's Park's early domination of the competition had any team won the trophy three years in succession. The club's official handbook said the feat would probably never be equalled. But it was. And the next team to equal it was Rangers 14 years later. The greatness of Struth's side was well and truly measured at Hampden that day.

That season, however, saw the departure of one of Ibrox's great favourites, Sandy Archibald, who returned to Raith Rovers. And on 22 April 1936 Davie Meiklejohn played his 635th, and last, game, against Hearts at Ibrox.

But there were still more triumphs for Struth's team before the outbreak of War as they lifted the title in 1936-7 under the captaincy of Jimmy Simpson. Surprisingly they were ousted from the cup at the first hurdle by Queen of the South, when centre-forward John Renwick inflicted the killer blow. It was Rangers' first defeat in 21 Scottish Cup matches.

In the last season before the Second World War, Rangers won their 24th title by a massive eleven points from Celtic. And it was against Celtic on 2 January 1939 that Ibrox's record attendance of 118,567 was set. But if 1938-9 was for breaking records and winning championships, it was also the end of an era. As with so many outstanding talents, the War also finished the playing days of the club's most prolific goalscorer, Bob McPhail.

Struth knew another rebuilding programme would be necessary if he was to maintain the level of consistency that had won Rangers 15 league titles and six Scottish Cup honours since the First World War.

Youngsters were introduced to the team as the Thirties came to a close. Willie Thornton made his debut against Partick Thistle in 1937 and the following year teenager Willie Waddell scored on his debut in the annual confrontation with Arsenal. Other newcomers were Scot Symon, Jimmy Duncanson, Willie Woodburn and Jock 'Tiger' Shaw. These men were to be the backbone of the next great Rangers side after the War.

Struth was a great admirer of the Arsenal side of the 1930s. He had struck up a relationship with the London club and an annual match started in the 1933-4 season. Struth adopted the Arsenal style of play with a stopper centre-half, and entrusted the role to Jimmy Simpson before the War. It was ironic that, in the six meetings between the two great clubs between 1933 and 1938, Arsenal never beat Rangers. This system was the start of Rangers' new defensive strategy that became known as the 'Iron Curtain'. It was to produce even greater post-War success.

The Iron Curtain and Beyond

Preceding pages *Jock 'Tiger' Shaw is chaired off by his team-mates after captaining Rangers to victory over Clyde in the 1949–50 Scottish Cup final – thus becoming the first club to achieve the Treble.*

Even with soccer curtailed during the War, Rangers still managed to show their dominance. They won the Western Division title in 1939–40 and were six-times winners of the Southern League, which was the First Division in all but name. On top of that they appeared in all six Southern League Cup finals, winning four. They won the Glasgow Cup five times as well. Admittedly, much of Rangers' success can be attributed to the fact that most of their players worked in 'essential industries' during the War and, consequently, were available for selection on Saturday afternoons. One notable exception was Willie Thornton. Because of his army service he only played a handful of games. Heady days returned in 1945 when the touring Moscow Dynamo side made Ibrox one of their ports of call during their British tour. A tremendously fit and imaginative side, Dynamo, under the guidance of coach Mikhail Yakushin, started their four-match British tour with a 3-3 draw against Chelsea at Stamford Bridge. The crowd of around 90,000 broke down the gates and flooded the vast stadium in an effort to get a glimpse of the Soviet side. Cardiff City were then to feel the full force of the Russians, who romped to a 10-1 victory. A strong Arsenal side, reinforced by Stanley Matthews, went down 4-3 at a fog-bound White Hart Lane (Arsenal's own ground was in War service). But then Dynamo headed north of the border to play one of the best British teams of the day, Rangers.

Played on a midweek afternoon, the game was all-ticket. The whole of Glasgow wanted to see the Russian team and the 90,000 limit was considerably short of the demand for a place on the Ibrox terracing.

The game (see page 106) ended at 2-2 and the capacity crowd was treated to great skills by both sides. The Russians were quick to point out that Rangers were the best team they played on their four-match tour.

The key to Rangers' success in the early post-War years was their solid defence, the so-called 'Iron Curtain'. The two men who formed its backbone were Willie Woodburn and George Young. Woodburn had joined them from Ashton Juveniles in 1937. He went on to become one of Scotland's classiest centre-halves and was capped 24 times.

Young was a giant of a man in every respect. He stood over six feet and weighed more than 15 stone. However, despite his size he was light on his

Right *Threat from the East: four Moscow Dynamos players on a walkabout in Glasgow before their epic match with Rangers in November 1945.*

30

Scot Symon, a strong defender, had spells with Rangers, Dundee and Portsmouth before moving into management.

feet and had deft ball control. He was to be the most commanding figure in Rangers' defences for more than 15 years. Scotland capped him 75 times in full and War-time internationals and he was honoured with the captaincy 50 times. He joined Rangers from Kirkintilloch Rob Roy in 1941. Within 18 months he was in the Scotland team.

Some of the old faces had gone; Jerry Dawson's time was up between the sticks and he was replaced by Bobby Brown, who made the short move from Queen's Park. Brown struggled to win over the Ibrox fans at first – but that was hardly surprising in view of Dawson's long tenure as Rangers' 'keeper. Other new faces included wing-half Sammy Cox and left back Jock Shaw, who was the club skipper. But as well as Bob McPhail, top goalscorer Jimmy Smith was no longer a regular first-teamer, and was to be given a free transfer at the end of the season.

When league soccer resumed in 1946, Rangers, with their new defence, were favourites to retain the 'A' Division title they had won in the last season before the War. And they did not disappoint their loyal fans. This time, however, they had new pretenders to their 'crown'. Celtic's challenge had waned and the men from Easter Road, Hibernian, were to chase Rangers all the way before the Light Blues won the title by two points.

Hibs had the better of the personal duels that season. They won the league game at Ibrox and drew at Easter Road. They also put Rangers out of the Scottish Cup in the second round. Rangers gained revenge in the new League Cup, winning 3-1 at Hampden in the semi-final before a crowd of more than 125,000. They went on to become the first winners of the new trophy when they beat Aberdeen 4-0 in the final.

Those meetings were to signal the start of many great confrontations between Rangers and Hibs in the early post-War years. They dominated Scottish soccer in the first seven years, with Rangers winning the league four times and Hibs three.

In 1948 Hibs turned the tables by taking the title, by two points, with Rangers in second place. The battles in those days between Rangers' 'Iron Curtain' and Hibs' brilliant 'Famous Five' forward line of Smith, Johnstone, Reilly, Turnbull and Ormond packed grounds whenever the two teams met. When they were drawn to meet in the Scottish Cup semi-final a massive 143,570 packed into Hampden. Rangers won that day; and they went on to beat Morton in the final after a replay – but what a fight of it the Greenock men made. Rangers scored their winning goal in the dying minutes of extra time when schoolteacher Billy Williamson, playing his first Scottish Cup game of the season, headed home a magnificent goal. Williamson had come into the team as a replacement for Willie Findlay, who had played in the first game which ended 1-1. For the replay a massive 129,176 passed through the Hampden turnstiles. It was a record for a midweek game in Britain – and an estimated 20,000 were locked out.

Having been obliged to acknowledge Hibs' superiority in 1948, Rangers showed total dominance the following season. They beat Raith Rovers 2-0 in the final to win the League Cup, beat Clyde 4-1 to win the Scottish Cup (Williamson again playing his only cup game of the season in the final), and also clinched the league title by one point from Dundee. Under skipper 'Tiger' Shaw they became the first club to win all three competitions in one season. Since then, they have emulated this feat on three occasions. (Celtic have performed the treble twice). But clinching the league title race that season was in the balance until the last kick of the season. As they went into the final Saturday Dundee were one point ahead of Rangers. The Light Blues were away to bottom club Albion Rovers, while Dundee had a tricky match at Falkirk. The Light Blues had no problems and won 4-1. They then had to sit nervously in the dressing room and await the result from Brockville. Then it came through. Falkirk had won 4-1 and Rangers were champions for the 26th time.

Thornton scored 36 goals that season, more than 20 of them with his head. He had developed a great partnership with right-winger Willie Waddell and they became noted for their one-twos. Behind them the half-back trio of Willie Woodburn, Sammy Cox and Ian McColl were the powerhouse of the great team. Like today's midfield 'generals', they were the motivators who set up attacks. But unlike most of today's midfielders, they also came back and tackled with ferocity. This was a great Rangers team, well-blended but with no superstars. They also had a strong back-up in a reserve side bristling with talent.

The 'Iron Curtain' conceded only 26 goals as Rangers retained the league title in 1949–50. But once more it was a close thing as they pipped free-scoring Hibs by one point. They clinched the title in the final match after nervously holding on for a 2-2 draw with Third Lanark at Cathkin Park. Third's outside right, Henderson, missed a penalty which would have given the league title to Hibs. Once more the Light Blues' strength lay in their defence, whose members were virtually ever-present, missing only two league games between them. In the League Cup East Fife gained their first-ever victory over Rangers when they won 2-1 in the semi-final at Hampden, but Rangers gained ample revenge by beating the Fifers 3-0 in the Scottish Cup six months later. Billy Williamson missed the final this time . . . and that was after playing in every round!

The following season, alarm bells were ringing around Ibrox. Apart from the Charity Cup, the trophy cabinet was bare. They were 10 points (and 14 goals) behind Hibernian in the league, they had been dumped out of the cup in the 2nd round, also by Hibs, and they had failed to reach the quarter-finals of the League Cup after two defeats by Aberdeen.

Was the Struth magic fading after all these years?

It certainly seemed to be in the 1951–2 season, when Hibs won the league again. This time the margin of victory was only four points but the 'Famous Five' scored 92 goals, whereas Rangers could muster only 61. There was further disappointment in the League Cup, when Dundee won the final 3-2 at Hampden to win their first honour since 1910.

Just as Rangers were being written off, they came back to prevent a Hibs hat-trick of league titles when they won on goal average in the 1952–3 season. Willie Waddell scored the equaliser in the 1-1 draw at Queen of the South in the final game of the season which secured the title. Rangers completed their seventh double when they beat Aberdeen 1-0 after a 1-1 draw in the Scottish Cup. But the changing face of the team was evident: only Young, Woodburn and McColl remained from the team which had lifted the trophy just three years earlier.

The following season, it really was to be the end of the Struth era. Rangers finished fourth in the League. They had not finished that low since 1926. Had they not had a better goal average than Hibernian, East Fife, Dundee and Clyde, they could well have finished ninth, which would have been the club's lowest-ever position. In the Scottish Cup they were hammered 6-0 by Aberdeen. It was the first (and only) time anybody has put six past the Light Blues in the competition.

By now Struth was in his late 70s and he reluctantly stood down for a younger man at the end of the season. He had guided the club through its greatest era and was responsible for 18 Championships, 10 Scottish Cup triumphs and two League Cup wins during his 34 years in charge. Those close to him predicted that, without Rangers, his life would hardly be worth living. And so it proved: two years after his retirement Struth died at the age of 81.

On 15 June 1954 Struth's successor was announced, largely on the recommendation of Struth himself. The person seen as the creator of the next great Rangers side was James Scotland Symon, known simply as Scot. Hailing from Errol in Perthshire, Symon was a good cricketer (he had played for Scotland). As a footballer he had played for Rangers, Dundee and Portsmouth, and had a reputation for being a tough tackler. As a manager he had built up a fine team at unfashionable East Fife before moving south of the border to join Preston in 1953. In his only full season at Deepdale he took the club to Wembley, where they lost 3-2 to West Bromwich Albion in the FA Cup final. Shortly afterwards he had talks with Rangers and had no hesitation in accepting one of the most prestigious jobs in British football.

Obviously Symon had a difficult job in following Struth but, perhaps fortunately, Struth's last great team was starting to break up. Jock Shaw and Willie Thornton decided to call it a day and so Symon had to go into the transfer market. In his first season Symon introduced 18-year-old Alex Scott into the team. Scott joined Rangers from Bo'ness in January 1955 and on his Rangers debut, at home to Falkirk, he made an impact with a hat-trick. A regular thereafter, he played his part in helping the team to finish third in

Scot Symon succeeded Struth in the manager's chair at Ibrox in 1954 and in 13 years built some of Rangers' finest post-war teams.

33

Preceding pages *Graeme Souness's inauspicious start to his first full season as Rangers' player-manager. Here he is surrounded by Hibs players after his tackle on George McCluskey in a League match at Easter Road in August 1986. Already booked, Souness was sent off for this offence.*

the league behind Aberdeen (who became champions for the first time in their history) and Celtic.

But Symon was building, and he set his sights on Europe. Rangers' first floodlighting system had already been installed, and on 8 December 1953 Arsenal played in the inaugural match under the Ibrox lights. The Londoners won 2-1. Lights were an essential part of European qualification even in those days. There had been talk of a European competition for league champions (the European Cup), and Symon, like Matt Busby, made that a personal target. In 1954–55, before the European Cup was first played, Symon arranged floodlit matches for Rangers against teams like Arsenal, Manchester City, Rapid Vienna and Racing Club de Paris.

Symon's first season in charge was not an easy one. It was not made any easier when Woodburn was sent off at the start of the season. It was the fourth dismissal of his career. His previous ban had been for six weeks, but this time the Scottish FA dropped a bombshell by suspending Willie Woodburn *sine die*. After three unsuccessful pleas to get the ban lifted he was eventually allowed back in April 1957. But at 37 he was too old. So, after 17 years and nearly 500 games for the club, another great player had, in effect, been lost to the new manager in his first season.

With Woodburn out of the side, Symon switched George Young to centre-half. One of the new faces in the team was Jimmy Millar, who Symon purchased from Dunfermline midway through the season for £5000. At the

Right *Jim Baxter – 'Slim Jim' to the idolizing Ibrox faithful – was signed by Scot Symon in 1960. The most extravagantly gifted player ever to wear a Rangers shirt, Baxter – like Alex James, a player of comparable genius in the 1930s – played his early League football for Raith Rovers. And like 'Wembley Wizard' James, Baxter took a particular delight in humbling the English: his performances in Scotland's victories at Wembley in 1963 and 1967 are still remembered with awe and astonishment by all who witnessed them.*

A less happy moment for Scotland in the 1963 Wembley match: Rangers' gifted full-back Eric Caldow is put on a stretcher after breaking a leg when tackling England's centre-forward Bobby Smith. Jim Baxter (at left) helps to comfort his clubmate.

end of the season Alex Murray was signed from Queen's Park, and £12,000 secured inside forward Sammy Baird from Preston North End, where Symon had been manager in 1953–4.

The glory days returned in 1955–6 as Rangers won the League from Aberdeen with six points to spare. The defence was seemingly unaffected by Woodburn's departure and conceded only 27 goals in 34 games. It had been significantly bolstered by Eric Caldow, who had become a regular in the team. The diminutive Caldow was not the strongest of tacklers but had outstanding positional sense. The attack didn't do too badly either, and it was the South African duo of centre-forward Don 'The Rhino' Kichenbrand and winger Johnny Hubbard who did most of the damage with 61 goals during the season.

Winning the league meant Symon could set out on his quest for European glory, and on 24 October 1956 Rangers lined up for their first game in the European Cup against Nice at Ibrox. Murray and Simpson scored Rangers' goals as they won the first leg 2-1 in front of 59,000 fans. The second leg at Nice attracted a mere 8,439 fans and when Hubbard scored a first-half penalty it looked as though Rangers were on their way into the second round. But Nice came back with two goals in two minutes to win 2-1 and thus force a third game. This was played at a neutral ground in Paris. Nice won 3-1, and Symon's dream came to an abrupt end.

Despite the defeat, Symon and Rangers learned a lot from the three matches. They realised how important a big first-leg lead at home is, and they learned that continental refereeing was inclined to be different, if not necessarily worse, than the best examples back home. However, in domestic competition the Light Blues won their 30th league title in 1956–7 after an unbeaten run of 16 matches pulled them away from Hearts who had led the table for most of the season. This enabled Rangers to get back into Europe immediately. The club's second campaign was to be without stalwart George Young, who announced his retirement during the 1957 close season after playing his last match in the Charity Cup semi-final against Clyde. So, after 678 games in the light-blue shirt, the 'Big Fella' retired. He was a very hard act to follow.

Preceding pages *Rangers'
keeper Chris Woods and defender
Jimmy Nicholl combine to foil
Celtic's Owen Archdeacon and
Paul McStay in the 1986 Skol
Cup final.*

Right *Davie White, previously
Clyde's manager and then Scot
Symon's assistant, was appointed
Rangers manager in November
1967 after Symon resigned.*

The second European campaign saw Rangers beat St Etienne 4-3 on
aggregate in the preliminary round, but the Italian giants AC Milan were
much too good for the Light Blues in the next round, which they won 6-1 on
aggregate after a resounding 4-1 first leg win at Ibrox in front of 85,000 fans.
Rangers had naively surrendered the home leg after leading with only 15
minutes to go.

The quest for European glory took its toll as Rangers finished 13 points
behind Hearts, who lost only once and scored a record 132 goals in the
league. In the League Cup final at Hampden, Celtic thrashed Rangers 7-1!

With the introduction of the new half-back pairing of Harold Davis and
Billy Stevenson, Rangers were back on top in 1958–59, when they
prevented a Hearts League double by taking their 31st title from the
Tynecastle team by two points. After they had made a poor start to the
season, they paid £10,000 for inside-forward Ian McMillan from
Airdrieonians. Thereafter the results improved.

The 1959–60 season was a mixed one for manager Symon. Rangers
finished third in the league behind Hearts and Kilmarnock (and trailed
Hearts' goal tally of 102 by 30 goals). Poor home form in the second half of
the season cost them dearly: in their last eight matches at Ibrox in the league
they didn't manage a single win. However, Symon enjoyed his first Scottish
Cup triumph when they beat Kilmarnock 2-0, with Millar scoring both goals
– and they could afford Eric Caldow's missing a penalty, just after half-time.

In Europe, Rangers took another step towards their dream, reaching the
semi-finals of the Champions' Cup. But Eintracht Frankfurt spoilt any
celebrations they might have planned, with two emphatic wins.

Rangers were not in the same class as their German opponents, who won
12-4 on aggregate after wins of 6-1 in Frankfurt and 6-3 at Ibrox. Eintracht
were an impressive side. But when they played Real Madrid in the greatest-
ever European Cup final, at Hampden Park, even they were made to look
mediocre by the likes of Di Stéfano and Puskás.

However, a player who, at his peak, would grace any World XI was
waiting in the wings. Earlier in the season Symon had tried to sign young
Jim Baxter from Raith Rovers, but a £12,000 bid was rejected. However,
after increasing the offer to £17,500 in the close season he landed his man.

Baxter's towering natural ability and marvellous arrogance soon made him a firm favourite with the Ibrox fans. 'Slim Jim' was the man Symon saw as the last vital cog in the wheel that was going to make Rangers great again. Baxter had complete mastery of the ball and his strolling gait concealed quicksilver creative vision. Irrespective of results, he brought the unmistakable stamp of sheer class back to Ibrox.

With Baxter marshalling the midfield and the goalscoring trio of Jimmy Millar, Dave Wilson and Ralph Brand, Rangers were champions for the 32nd time in 1960–1, when they pipped Kilmarnock by one point. Kilmarnock also provided the opposition for Rangers in the League Cup final, but the trophy came to Ibrox after a 2-0 win. Any hopes of winning all three major domestic trophies vanished in the third round of the Scottish Cup when Motherwell had an amazing 5-2 win at Ibrox. But in the Cup-Winners' Cup Rangers had their greatest European moment to date.

After beating Ferencvaros 5-4 on aggregate they dumped Borussia Mönchengladbach 11-0. In the Ibrox leg Rangers won 8-0, and Brand scored a hat-trick. After beating Wolves, then the pride of English football, in the semi-final, Rangers met the Italian club Fiorentina in the two-legged final.

Jimmy Millar was unfit for the first leg at Ibrox, and to make matters worse Rangers Eric Caldow missed a penalty. Fiorentina won the leg 2-0 thanks to two goals from Milan. Rangers found the defensive skill of the Italians too difficult to break down and Fiorentina won the second leg 2-1. So, European glory was still just a dream for Rangers. But the three seasons between 1962–64 saw the great days of the 1920s return to Ibrox.

Second to Dundee in the league in 1961–2, a disastrous run-in to the end of the season cost Rangers dearly. But they did win both the Scottish Cup and League Cup, beating St Mirren and Hearts respectively. Into the team had come new talent in the shape of forwards John Greig and Willie Henderson. Both turned out to be Ibrox stalwarts over the years.

The following season Rangers ran away with the league, nine points ahead of Kilmarnock, one of only two teams to beat them (the other was Dundee United). The Scottish Cup also made its way back to Ibrox after the 3-0 demolition of Celtic in the replayed final at Hampden, thanks to two goals from Brand and one from Wilson.

There were several shuffles amongst the playing staff in 1962–3. Liverpool signed Billy Stevenson, Alex Scott moved to Everton, and Max

Old Ibrox favourites David Kinnear and Willie Thornton in the dugout as Rangers beat Dundee United in a League match in December 1969.

41

Preceding pages *Rangers*
striker Ally McCoist celebrates
after scoring a hat-trick in an
April 1987 League match against
Hearts.

Murray joined West Brom, while George McLean came from St Mirren.

Rangers retained the championship in 1964 and Symon's men went on to emulate Bill Struth's team of 1948–9 and win all three major titles in one season. They secured the League Cup with a resounding 5-0 win over second division Morton. All five goals were scored in the second half, Jim Forrest scoring four and his cousin Alec Willoughby the other. In the Scottish Cup, the 120,000 fans were anticipating extra time until Millar and Brand scored two goals in the last minute to take the Cup to Ibrox for the third year in succession. Eric Caldow had missed most of the 1963–4 season after breaking his leg in three places following a collision with England's Bobby Smith after only six minutes of the international at Wembley in April 1963.

By now Symon had completely rebuilt the Rangers side, and had successfully carried on where Struth left off. Only success in Europe could prove how great they were. But it was that thirst for glory that ended in disaster at the Prater Stadium, Vienna, one December day in 1964.

Rangers were defending a 1-0 home leg lead in the European Cup against Rapid Vienna. Forrest and Wilson scored two goals in the away leg and Rangers were coasting comfortably into the next round. Jim Baxter, who had played what many regard as the greatest ever individual performance in a Rangers shirt, was tackled from behind by Skocik in the final minute. He lay on the Austrian turf with a fractured leg. Baxter was out of training for two months and on his return to the side his enthusiasm and motivation had gone. At the end of the season, after Rangers finished fifth in the League, Symon sold Baxter to Sunderland for £72,000.

In just five years at Rangers Baxter had been involved with three championship, three Scottish Cup and four League Cup-winning teams. A lot of Rangers' success in that period can be attributed to 'Slim Jim's' tremendous creative drive.

Overall, 1964–5 was a bad season for Rangers. Willie Henderson was out of action for most of the season with bunion trouble; Hibernian knocked them out of the Scottish Cup in the third round and three goals in three minutes by Inter Milan at the San Siro stadium dented their European Cup hopes. However, a couple of bright spots emerged in the season: Baxter masterminded a 2-1 win over Celtic in the League Cup final, and a new

Right *Willie Waddell, one of*
Rangers' favourite sons,
succeeded Davie White at Ibrox
in 1969, after guiding
Kilmarnock to success in the late
Fifties and Sixties. Here he
organises a squad portrait in
1970. Later Waddell became
General Manager and then a
director of the club.

goal-scoring sensation was found in Jim Forrest. Playing his first full season as a successor to Jimmy Millar, Forrest netted the two goals that beat Celtic. But they were just two of the 57 he scored in all domestic and European matches, including 30 in 30 league games.

The following season saw the emergence of Celtic as the new giants of Scottish football – and their dominance was to last for almost a decade. Under new manager Jock Stein they beat Rangers into second place in the league: after a season-long battle the Light Blues were edged out by two points. The two teams scored 197 goals between them in 68 matches. Defending champions Kilmarnock were 10 points adrift of Rangers.

Celtic also had the upper hand in the League Cup, winning the final 2-1 in front of 107,000 at Hampden. But Rangers achieved sweet revenge in the Scottish Cup. After a goalless draw in front of 126,000 fans, a single goal from full back Kai Johansen, a pre-season signing from Morton, 20 minutes from time took the Cup to Ibrox for the 19th time. The two games attracted a total of more than 225,000 fans.

Despite winning the Cup, Scot Symon was now under the greatest pressure since he first took charge at Ibrox. Something had to be done to stop Celtic, who had made the 'breakthrough'. Dave Smith was bought from Aberdeen and Alex Smith from Dunfermline for a combined fee of £80,000. Alex Smith was to be the top goalscorer in 1966–7. But on 28 January 1967 disaster struck when Rangers suffered the greatest humiliation in their history. They were drawn away to second division Berwick Rangers in the Scottish Cup, and it was impossible to anticipate anything but a Rangers win. But the 'impossible' happened: Berwick won 1-0 thanks to a Sammy Reid goal in the 35th minute. It was the first time since Queen of the South had beaten them 1-0 in 1936–7 that Rangers had been eliminated in the 1st round. Sweeping changes were made; McLean and Forrest were transferred while Andy Penman, who came to Rangers as part of the deal that took McLean to Dundee, and Sandy Jardine provided new faces and talents.

The Light Blues pride was dented even further as Celtic consolidated their position at the top of Scottish football.

Celtic beat Rangers 1-0 in the 1966–7 League Cup final, despite some dubious refereeing; and they scored 111 goals in winning the League by

Derek Johnstone (9) celebrates after scoring the only goal in Rangers' League Cup final victory over Celtic at Hampden in October 1970. Also on hand are Alex Miller (left) and Alfie Conn.

three points from Rangers (who scored 92). Then, having won the Scottish Cup final against Aberdeen, Celtic provided the biggest jolt to the Ibrox players, management, and fans. They did what Scot Symon had been trying to do for 12 years, becoming the first UK club to win the European Cup.

Less than a week after Celtic beat Inter Milan, Rangers had a great chance to make it a Glasgow double when they lined up against Bayern Munich in the Cup-Winners' Cup final at Nuremberg. After a goalless 90 minutes the 'home' team ended up the eventual winners thanks to a solitary goal scored by West German international Roth four minutes into the second period of extra time. So it was elation at Parkhead; despair at Ibrox.

Alex Ferguson, bought from Dunfermline for £65,000; Swedish winger Orjan Persson, who came from Dundee United in a deal that took the long-serving Davie Wilson the other way; and Danish international 'keeper Erik Sorensen were recruited at the start of the 1967–8 season. But they did little to change the fortunes of Rangers.

Despite scoring 93 goals and losing only one match, they still had to watch Celtic take the Championship for the third successive year. Moreover, Celtic prevented them from reaching the knockout stage of the League Cup, and Hearts inflicted the knockout blow in the third round of the Scottish Cup. Any chance of salvaging something from Europe disappeared when Leeds United knocked the Light Blues out 2-0 on aggregate in the quarter-final of the Inter-Cities Fairs Cup. So that was it: complete failure.

Davie White, the Clyde manager, had been appointed Symon's assistant and many saw this as a move to oust Symon from the manager's chair. And indeed they were right because on 1 November 1967 it was announced that Symon had quit and was to be replaced by White, who became the club's fourth manager in 68 years. Twelve months earlier White had been a part-time player with Clyde!

Right *Willie Johnstone tangles with Moscow Dynamo defender Zukov in the epic European Cup-Winners' Cup final at Barcelona in May 1972.*

Many thought White was not experienced enough for the job, and there were many who had doubts about his ability to take charge of such a great team. But at the time Rangers were reduced to clutching at straws. A depression had set in, and Celtic were monopolising the game: Rangers were now living in the shadow of Parkhead. For a club that had enjoyed so much success over the years, that situation could not be tolerated.

White silenced his critics by chasing Celtic all the way to the Championship in his first season. But, for the third successive year, they finished runners-up to their great rivals. Defeat in the final match at Aberdeen cost Rangers dearly.

The following season White was joined by Willie Thornton who quit as Partick Thistle manager to return to Ibrox as assistant manager. White then splashed out a Scottish record £100,000 on striker Colin Stein from Hibernian, and a further £50,000 for St Johnstone's Alex MacDonald. Stein had an immediate impact, scoring hat tricks in his first two matches. But a seven-match ban on him at the end of the season did little to help Rangers' cause as they surrendered the title.

Rangers fans celebrate after the match in Barcelona.

Celtic also prevented progress in the League Cup; and in the Scottish Cup final Rangers were no match for the sheer class of their Parkhead rivals who ran out comfortable winners 4-0. A good win over Athletic Bilbao in the quarter-final of the Fairs Cup set them on course to salvage something from an otherwise dismal season, but eventual champions Newcastle United beat them 2-0 over the two legs.

Ibrox was rapidly becoming a depressing place to be. The cheque book had failed to bring success back to the club. Even the return of the prodigal son, Jim Baxter, did not help. And the day after losing 1-3 at home to Gornik Zabrze in the Cup-Winners' Cup in November 1969 Davie White was told his days in charge were over.

But who would be the man to succeed White? There was no doubt a man of powerful personality and able to command respect, like Willie Struth and Scot Symon, was required. The likely candidate was Willie Waddell. A former favourite with the Ibrox fans, they certainly wanted him back. But he had turned his back on the game and was enjoying a new career in journalism. He met the directors, and on 3 December 1969 it was announced that Willie Waddell would be the next manager of Glasgow Rangers. Was this the dawning of another great era for the club?

He used the first season as one of consolidation. Celtic won the title yet again – and this time Rangers were 12 points adrift – but Waddell had spent his first half-season carefully monitoring the playing and backroom staff. In the close season he made sweeping changes to his coaching staff. Out went Davie Kinnear after 26 years with the club. Willie Thornton, however, was retained as assistant manager and the appointment of Jock Wallace, the Hearts assistant manager, as first-team coach was one of several new moves. Three years earlier Wallace had been in goal for Berwick when they had that historic cup win over the Light Blues.

Waddell and Wallace instilled confidence and determination into the players. Their hard work was rewarded instantly as Rangers beat Celtic to win the League Cup. A brilliant debut goal by 16-year-old Derek Johnstone, playing in his first ever cup-tie, brought the first trophy to come to Ibrox for five years.

The lack of consistency saw Rangers finish fourth in the League but they did reach the Scottish Cup final. Johnstone scored the equaliser three minutes from time that earned a replay, but two quick goals by Celtic in the second match finished off Rangers, who went down 2-1.

But the 1970–71 season was not about winning or losing. it was about the

Colin Stein, a highly accomplished striker, had two periods at Ibrox. His first, from 1968 to 1972, was followed by three years with Coventry City. Here he is in determined mood against Motherwell in one of his first League games after his return to Ibrox in 1975.

biggest disaster to hit British football. Eighty thousand fans packed Ibrox for the New Year Old Firm clash. Celtic were leading 2-1 as the match came to a close. Thousands of fans were on their way out of the ground when up went a roar. Rangers had equalised through Colin Stein. Many of those fans turned to get back onto the terracing to share the moment of joy. But disaster: one fan slipped and suddenly there was a mass of bodies. Sixty-six people died and 145 more were injured. The tragedy was felt by people all over the world.

Wadell had to pick everyone up for the 1971–2 season. Another trophy would be the best tonic, but they bid farewell to the League after a dismal start which saw them lose four of their first five matches, and they failed to make the knockout stage of the League Cup. But in Europe Waddell was destined to fulfil Scot Symon's 17-year-old dream.

After beating the French club Rennes 2-1 on aggregate they faced the top Portuguese side Sporting Lisbon. Two goals from Stein and one from Henderson gave Rangers a 3-0 half-time lead in the home leg – which they wasted by letting Sporting score two second-half goals. The odds were firmly against the Light Blues.

After travel difficulties which resulted in Rangers taking a day and a half to reach Lisbon, few gave them any chance. Sporting led 2-1 at half-time and Rangers were hanging on. They levelled it at 2-all and were ahead once more on aggregate. But then Ronnie McKinnon broke his leg, and in the closing minutes Sporting equalised. The match went into extra time.

The tired legs of the Rangers players just kept going and their hard work seemed like being rewarded when Willie Henderson put them back in the lead but then Sporting equalised six minutes from time. It ended up 6-all and it went to a penalty shoot-out which Rangers lost. Then amid scenes of confusion, Waddell produced a UEFA rule book which showed that in such a match the extra-time goals of the away team counted double. The following day Rangers were confirmed as winners.

If Rangers were to prove themselves in Europe then their next opponents would be a true test of their ability: they had to travel to Italy to play the crack Turin side Torino. A 12th-minute goal from Willie Johnston boosted Rangers' confidence and then, for an hour, the defence held out magnificently against the barrage of Torino attacks. The Italians got an equaliser but it stayed at 1-1 and Rangers clinched the tie at Ibrox.

This they did when an Alex MacDonald goal just after the interval was enough to put them into the semi-final against Bayern Munich, who had such stars as Franz Beckenbauer and Gerd Müller in their ranks. Bayern had put Rangers out of the Fairs Cup the previous season after a controversial Müller goal at Ibrox. Now they had the chance to gain retribution.

Playing away in the first leg, the Light Blues had to come from behind to force a 1-1 draw. A place in the final was there for the taking and they pulled through 2-0 on the night (see page 110).

With the scalps of Sporting Lisbon, Torino and Bayern Munich to their credit, Rangers could go into the final in Barcelona with confidence. Waddell, however, knew his team must not get over confident. There was no way he was going to get this far and lose. The attendance at the Nou Camp Stadium was 24,701 – about 16,000 of them wore the blue and white of Rangers – and they saw Rangers gain their first European triumph (see page 112).

At the end, amidst scenes of chaos, the Rangers fans spilled on to the pitch to slap each of their heroes on the back and to get a glimpse of the trophy. The Spanish police were not prepared for such an invasion and drew batons in an effort to clear the pitch. The action of some foolhardy supporters, and the lack of restraint by the Spanish police, cost Rangers a year out of Europe (the ban was originally for two years but was later reduced to one).

The troubles on the pitch apart, that May day in 1972 heralded the start of a new era in the history of Glasgow Rangers. Two men were the inspiration behind the Ibrox revival: manager Waddell and John Greig, the best Rangers captain since Davie Meiklejohn. While Waddell did all the work

John Greig, perhaps Rangers most inspirational captain since Davie Meiklejohn, was a key member of Ibrox sides between 1960 and 1978. Originally an inside forward, he found his best position at left-half. In this picture he shows his defensive qualities as he tackles Motherwell's Graham in a 1970s League match.

Above *Alex MacDonald was one of Rangers' most relentless midfield dynamos in the early Seventies, with the knack of scoring rare but priceless goals. Here he is in action against Hearts in the 1976 Scottish Cup final, when he scored in the 3-1 victory.*

Right *A footballer of immense natural skill and elegance, Derek Johnstone could perform equally effectively at centre-forward or centre-half. He's seen here in the 1972 Cup-Winners' Cup final against Moscow Dynamo, when he scored two of Rangers' three goals.*

blending the team off the pitch, John Greig was the mastermind on the pitch. The two men deserved their success at Barcelona.

Waddell, recognising the great partnership he had built with his right-hand man Wallace, suggested to the board in the close season that he himself be elevated to a position of General Manager, to cope with the administrative side of the job, and that Wallace should be appointed team manager. The board accepted the idea and the club went into the 1972-3 campaign with continued optimism.

But the season started badly. They lost 4-1 at home to St Mirren in the League Cup, and opened their league programme with a defeat by Ayr United. Willie Johnston was banned for nine weeks from September and in October they sold Colin Stein to Coventry in a £100,000-plus deal.

Celtic went on to win their eighth consecutive championship, with Rangers just one point behind, but in the Scottish Cup they beat the Parkhead men 3-2 to win the cup for the first time in seven years. But the next season saw another drought at Ibrox. Willie Waddell's great job in reviving Rangers had been rewarded in the 1973 close season, when he was invited to join the board. But on the playing field it all went wrong.

Home defeats by Celtic, Hearts and East Fife by the beginning of October were to prove costly, and Celtic comfortably won the championship again. Celtic knocked the Light Blues out of the League Cup, and in the Scottish Cup Rangers lost at home to Dundee in the third round. Rangers were back in Europe but the top Germans Borussia Mönchengladbach played their part in making it a disastrous season for Rangers. On top of all that, Rangers failed to qualify for Europe in 1974-5. But not having any European commitment may have been a blessing in disguise.

Celtic had won the championship nine seasons in succession and Rangers had offered little in the way of a serious challenge in all those years. But now they had a team ready to win back the title. The youths that Waddell and Wallace had developed were now starting to mature fully.

By November Rangers were looking potential champions. They were unbeaten in their first 12 matches before Hibernian won at Ibrox in the 'unlucky' 13th match (Hibs had won at Ibrox a couple of months earlier to put the Light Blues out of the League Cup). But Rangers maintained their great run of success and lost only two more matches. Colin Stein, who returned to Ibrox from Coventry in an £80,000 deal in March, scored the equaliser against Hibs three weeks later that clinched Rangers' first title since 1963-4. It ended their longest run without a championship flag since the League was formed in 1890. One of the inspirations behind the success was Sandy Jardine, who was deservedly voted Scotland's Player of the Year.

The following season saw the introduction of the new Premier Division and Rangers retained the championship. But in addition, they added the Scottish Cup and League Cup to give Wallace his first treble, and the club's first for 12 years. A magnificent run of 21 games without defeat from the beginning of December steered the Ibrox men to a six-point victory over Celtic. It was also Celtic who were beaten by a 67th-minute Alex MacDonald goal in the League Cup final, but in the Scottish Cup Rangers looked like going out to Motherwell in the semi-final. Two down with 20 minutes to go, they drew level and then, in the last minute, Derek Johnstone scored the winner. In the final against Hearts, it was Johnstone who opened the scoring in the first minute as Rangers went on to win 3-1.

Under the leadership of John Greig, Rangers were once again the force they had been in the days of Struth and Symon. And yet, inexplicably, 1976-7 brought nothing but one failure after another.

With only one win from their first five league games, the now traditional

poor start to the season was too much of a handicap to overcome and Celtic took full advantage, eventually winning the title by nine points. In the League Cup there was a humiliating 5-1 semi-final defeat by Aberdeen. FC Zürich dumped them out of the European Cup in the first round. And to hammer the last nail into the coffin, Celtic won the Old Firm encounter in the Scottish Cup Final at Hampden with a Lynch penalty.

What had happened? Good players don't suddenly become bad players over a season. But to confuse the issue even further, Rangers followed up their disastrous 1976–7 season by completing the treble a year later! It was Wallace's second treble in three years, so the fans were prepared to forgive'n'forget that one lapse in between.

Rangers won the league by two points from Aberdeen but to make it even sweeter, Celtic languished 19 points behind the Light Blues in fifth place. It was the biggest gap between the two clubs since Rangers won the first division in 1947–8 with Celtic 23 points behind in 12th place. They also beat Celtic 2-1 to win the League Cup. New signing Gordon Smith from Kilmarnock scored the winner two minutes from the end of extra time. The treble was completed by beating Aberdeen 2-1 in the Scottish Cup.

Then came the traumatic announcement that Jock Wallace was quitting to take charge of Leicester City. He was replaced by the man who had just skippered the club to the treble, John Greig, who hung up his boots after a 16-year playing career that saw him play a club record 496 league games. They often said Greig was the man Rangers couldn't do without. Now they needed him more than ever after the shock of Wallace's departure. Greig appointed Derek Johnstone as team captain – and the new manager and skipper came close to another treble in the first season.

Gordon Smith (10) puts the ball past Motherwell keeper Rennie in a 1975 League match.

Alex MacDonald and John Greig (left) in action during the 1976 Scottish Cup final against Hearts.

They won the League Cup by beating Aberdeen 2-1 in a stirring last 13 minutes when they scored their two goals. Alex MacDonald equalised and then Jackson scored the winner in injury time. Greig had wasted little time in emulating the great managers of the past and brought instant success to the club. The league was a close-run affair between the two Glasgow giants. Rangers lost out to Celtic by just three points and the game that took the title to Parkhead was the third from last game of the season, which Celtic won 4-2.

But that disappointment was overcome at Hampden a few weeks later when, at the third attempt, Rangers beat Hibernian 3-2 in extra time after two goalless draws, to win the Scottish Cup. Rangers' winner came from an own goal ten minutes from the end.

Greig's team also showed they were going to be a force in Europe once more when they had a great win over Juventus in the European Cup. It was only a couple of Dieter Müller goals in the quarter-final that saw Cologne go through to the semis 2-1 on aggregate.

Rangers continued their 'yo-yo' form in 1979–80 and failed to bring a trophy to the club. Willie Waddell resigned as managing director and vice-chairman at the beginning of the season, but remained as a consultant. Greig saw the need to introduce new faces into the team but this time there was not the depth in the reserves and he was heavily involved in the transfer market. He bought full back Gregor Stevens from Leicester in a £150,000 deal and then paid a Scottish record £210,000 to Dundee for Ian Redford. But the new signings could not bring the championship back to Ibrox, as Celtic won the title with Rangers in a sorry fifth place, having lost 14 of their 36 matches. This was the most defeats Rangers have ever suffered in the league in one season.

The only chance Greig had of salvaging something was at Hampden at the end of the season when they appeared in their fifth successive Scottish Cup final. It was yet another Old Firm encounter. After a goalless 90 minutes George McCluskey scored the only goal of the game in the second half of extra time to deprive Rangers of the trophy.

*Skipper Greig amid Rangers'
incredible hardware haul in
1975–6. From left: the League
Cup, Glasgow Cup, Reserves
League Championship Cup,
Scottish Cup, and Premier
Division Trophy.*

But changes were to be made, and at the end of the season Derek Parlane was sold to Leeds, Gordon Smith went to Brighton for £400,000 and Alex MacDonald, the man who had scored so many vital goals, went to Hearts for £30,000. In came Colin McAdam from Partick Thistle for £150,000 and another £180,000 brought Jim Bett from Belgium club Lokeren. Willie Johnston rejoined the club from Vancouver Whitecaps. With such activity in the transfer market there just had to be success again at Ibrox in 1980–1. But all they had to show for it was the Scottish Cup.

After a great start to the league (unbeaten in the first 15 matches) they fell away and finished third behind Celtic and Aberdeen. Aberdeen eliminated them in the League Cup and, not having any involvement in Europe, Rangers competed in the Anglo–Scottish Cup but suffered an embarrassing defeat by English Third Division side Chesterfield.

Their only consolation came in their sixth consecutive Scottish Cup Final. Their opponents were Dundee United, playing in only their second final. Redford missed a penalty for Rangers with the last kick of normal time and after a further 30 minutes it was still goalless. In the replay, however, Rangers played brilliantly to build up a 3-1 half time lead before running out the easy 4-1 winners.

The following season Redford was the Rangers hero when he scored the winning goal two minutes from time to beat United 2-1 in the League Cup final to prevent the Taysiders from completing a hat-trick of wins. But that success was all Greig got out of his fourth season in charge. Matters were not eased when Gregor Stevens received a six-month ban after being sent off for the fifth time in his career.

Although they could finish only third in the league, Rangers had hopes of completing a cup double. But Aberdeen showed little respect in the Scottish Cup final and scored three goals in extra time for a 4-1 win.

The club was now having to live in the shadow of Aberdeen as well as of Celtic. Once more Rangers found themselves at the crossroads. Admittedly there had been a trophy of some sort come to Ibrox each season, but since doubles and trebles had been commonplace at one time, one trophy seemed hardly better than routine. And in 1983 there was not even one trophy to adorn the showcase.

Despite further transfer activity, Greig could not get the blend right for a championship-winning team. Tommy McLean quit playing to become Greig's assistant. They paid £100,000 to Malmö for midfielder Robert Prytz, and then laid out a club record £225,000 to bring Craig Paterson from Hibernian in an effort to tighten up the defence. Towards the end of the season they paid West Ham £160,000 for striker Sandy Clark. The result of all that: fourth in the league (18 points behind champions Dundee United) and runners-up in the two cup competitions.

In the League Cup it was Celtic who took the trophy after a 2-1 win. In the Rangers side that day was Gordon Smith, back at Ibrox on loan. Later in the season he appeared in the FA Cup final at Wembley for Brighton – but it led to another loser's medal for him. Rangers reached their eighth successive Scottish Cup final but Aberdeen, once more, spoilt the celebrations when Eric Black scored the only goal of the game four minutes from the end of extra time.

Rangers' challenge in Europe had waned in recent years and 1982–3 was no exception. After beating Borussia Dortmund in the UEFA Cup, they played the other West German side Cologne. After winning 2-1 at Ibrox,

Above *Inspirational manager Jock Wallace at a Rangers 1970s training session.*

Below *Gordon Smith (second left) scores Rangers' second goal in the March 1978 League Cup final against Celtic.*

57

Rangers then showed their vulnerability by conceding four goals in the first 21 minutes of the return leg; Cologne ran out 5-0 winners.

Greig knew the magnitude of his task if he was to put things right. Failure was not a word in the Ibrox vocabulary. At the end of the season he let Jim Bett go back to Belgium and bought Ally McCoist from Sunderland for £185,000. Rangers had tried to buy him a year earlier but their bid of £300,000 was £100,000 less than Sunderland's asking price.

On 22 October 1983 Rangers lost at home 2-1 to Motherwell. It was their fifth defeat in nine league games. Six days later John Greig resigned after 23 years with the club. Assistant Tommy McLean took temporary charge as the board set out to find the man who could restore the club to its former glory.

Alex Ferguson, who had turned Aberdeen into one of the leading European clubs, was an obvious choice. But he was not interested. Second choice Jim McLean, who had worked wonders at Dundee United, gave the board the same thumbs down. And so it was to their next choice – Jock Wallace.

The Motherwell manager was tempted back to Ibrox for his second term. Leaving Motherwell was a wrench for Wallace because he had made a lot of friends at Fir Park. But stepping into the hottest seat in Scottish football was too great a temptation. Wallace made sweeping changes as he hit Ibrox like a hurricane. Morale was rock bottom and he had to do something about it. The backroom team was changed; Alex Totten of Falkirk was brought in as assistant manager, and the respected coach John Hagart was also recruited.

Despite a 3-0 defeat by Aberdeen in his first game, a lot of hard work by Wallace and the players started to produce results. They lost only one more league game all season, 3-0 to Celtic at Parkhead. But the early season defeats

Colin Jackson (left) and Sandy Jardine battle for a high ball with Motherwell's Gregor Stevens in a 1977 League match.

were too big an obstacle to overcome and Rangers finished fourth, 15 points behind champions Aberdeen.

But the Wallace magic did work in the League Cup. They had a good 3-1 aggregate semi-final win over Dundee United to set up another Old Firm clash. Rangers twice led, through McCoist goals, but Celtic equalised each time. Their second goal came from a Mark Reid penalty in the last minute. As the game went into extra time Rangers were awarded a penalty in the last minute of the first half. McCoist stepped up and hit the ball directly at Bonner. But he followed up to complete his hat-trick and bring the trophy to Ibrox for the 12th time.

That was Rangers' only trophy, but in the European Cup-Winners' Cup they created a club (and Scottish) record when they beat Valetta of Malta 8-0 and 10-0 to record an 18-0 aggregate scoreline. In the next round they met top Portuguese team FC Porto. Coasting to a 2-0 first leg win, Rangers ruined their chances when goalkeeper McCloy made a dreadful error three minutes from time to give the visitors a vital away goal. Porto won the second leg 1-0 and that McCloy mistake proved very costly, the Portuguese ultimately going through to the final.

Rangers were having a problem finding the net. Their top league scorers were Sandy Clark and Ally McCoist with a mere nine goals each. Ted McMinn and Iain Ferguson were recruited to bolster the attack, while Cammy Fraser was bought from Dundee for £165,000 in an effort to improve the midfield.

Davie Cooper (right) fires in the first goal against Celtic in the 1978 League Cup final; Derek Johnstone takes evasive action.

The 1984–5 season started well, but a disastrous second half was their downfall. In the first 18 games they lost only twice; but the second 18 saw nine defeats and they finished 21 points behind champions Aberdeen.

The final of the League Cup, now re-named the Skol Cup, was as usual played in the first half of the season, which was fortunate bearing in mind Rangers' second-half form. They played a strong Dundee United side in dreadful conditions and the only goal of the game was scored a minute before the interval when Iain Ferguson hammered home a low shot. New captain Craig Paterson climbed the Hampden steps to collect the trophy and give hopes for a revival in Rangers' fortunes.

Ten days later Rangers gave one of their finest displays of the season when they beat the top Italian side Inter Milan 3-1 in the UEFA Cup. Sadly, the performance went unrewarded because Milan had won the first leg 3-0.

The win over Inter was to be the last game in a Rangers jersey for defender John McClelland. The following day he was transferred to Watford for £265,000. As Rangers were going through their second half slump, there came the news in April that Scot Symon had died at the age of 74. Oh, how they longed for the successful Symon era to return to Ibrox. . . .

But it didn't. In fact, things got worse. For the first time in 12 years, Rangers failed to win the championship or to reach either of the two major Cup finals. True, they beat Celtic to win the Glasgow Cup at the end of the season, but that was scant consolation for finishing fifth to the old enemy in the league, losing to Hearts at the first hurdle in the Scottish Cup, enduring a semi-final beating by Hibs in the Skol Cup, and succumbing to little-known Spaniards Osasuna in the first round of the UEFA Cup.

With no hope of salvaging anything from the season, Wallace departed by 'mutual agreement'. It came as no surprise in view of the results. His successor was announced at the same time as Wallace's dismissal. The new man would be Scotland's captain and iron man Gracme Souness, the first player/manager in the club's history.

Souness had never played for a Scottish club but he had great leadership qualities. And having spent six glorious years with Liverpool, there was no doubting he had the right pedigree.

The Souness Revolution

David Holmes, who is Chief Executive was mainly responsible for bringing Graeme Souness to Ibrox.

Preceding pages *Davie Cooper (arms raised) is greeted by Ally McCoist (9) after scoring the winning (penalty) goal against Celtic in the 1986 Skol Cup final. Celtic players (left to right) are Mo Johnston, Paul McStay and Paul McGugan (13).*

Right *Terry Butcher (centre) wins a high ball in the 1986 Skol Cup semi final against Dundee United. Team-mate Robert Fleck is at right; United's Kevin Gallacher at left. Rangers won 2-1.*

The appointment of Souness as Rangers manager was the most dramatic development in Scottish football since Jock Stein had taken over as Celtic boss some 20 years earlier.

Souness was a determined man; furthermore, he was a winner. And the man who had once won a 'Body Beautiful' competition at Butlin's, Ayr, knew the enormity of the task as he took over one of the biggest jobs in British soccer. Rangers had to pay Souness's Italian club Sampdoria £300,000 for his signature – but that would be peanuts if he could bring them success.

One of his first decisions was to announce that he would sign players irrespective of religion. Being married to a Catholic, Souness knew it would be hypocritical to operate any other policy. Such promises had come from Ibrox before, but this time they had a ring of truth. There was a new breed of people in control at the club and a new era was dawning. Chief Executive David Holmes was a visionary and he was prepared to back Souness all the way. He realised that Rangers fans were no longer interested in bigotry but wanted success. Gone were the days when a chairman (less than ten years earlier) was deposed from office after only 24 hours when it was realised that his late wife had been a Catholic.

Two months after Souness swept into Ibrox he announced that he had signed 15-year-old schoolboy John Spencer on a two-year contract. Souness meant what he had said: young Spencer was a Catholic.

Souness set up a new management team. Walter Smith, the assistant manager at Dundee United and to the Scottish national team, was brought in as the number two and Don McKay, the former Coventry City manager, came as coach. Smith looked after the team as caretaker until Souness took over three weeks after his appointment.

The new boss was in charge in time for the final league game of the season. More than 17,000 Ibrox fans saw Rangers sign off with a 2-0 win over Motherwell. It was their first win in six matches. But it was an important win because it guaranteed them a place in Europe.

With the season over, Souness sat down and worked out his campaign plan. He went to Watford and paid £175,000 for striker Colin West. That transfer had little significance at the time, but it was the start of a drain of English players across the border, the like of which had never been seen before in Scottish football history. England internationals Terry Butcher (Ipswich) and goalkeeper Chris Woods (Norwich) were also recruited and lined up for the first match of the 1986–7 season, at Hibernian.

All eyes were on Easter Road to see what kind of job Souness had done in the close season. After all, he had already spent £2 million south of the border. Pre-season friendlies suggested Souness had not got the blend right. There seemed to be a weakness in the full-back positions. After a defeat by Bayern Munich, a few days before the Hibs match, Souness brought West Brom's Jimmy Nicholl back to Ibrox in an exchange deal for Bobby Williamson. The scene was set. It was all-ticket at Easter Road. But the outcome was a disaster, both for Rangers and for Souness personally. After 23 minutes he was booked for a tackle on Hibs captain Kirkwood. Fifteen minutes later the Rangers boss received his marching orders after a vicious tackle on George McCluskey, who required nine stitches in a gashed knee. A free-for-all broke out in the middle of the field. All players except Hibernian goalkeeper Alan Rough were involved. The scenes prompted a Scottish FA inquiry and Souness's great day was one of shame. To add to the misery, Hibs won 2-1. Ten days later the SFA fined Rangers £5,000 and Hibernian £1,000 for their parts in the fracas.

After beating Falkirk with a McCoist penalty in the next match, Rangers

then lost to Dundee United who won for the first time in 13 matches at Ibrox. With 20 minutes to go Rangers were coasting to a 2-0 win. Twenty minutes later, having lost 3-2, Souness had to listen to chants of 'what a load of rubbish' from the Ibrox terraces. It appeared that the huge investment in the transfer market had been a failure.

By the end of October, however, the early season traumas were forgotten and Rangers were running smoothly. They were lying third in the league and had reached the final of the Skol Cup. And once again it was an Old Firm showdown.

Souness already had a great record against Celtic. He had been in charge when Rangers beat them 3-2 after extra time in the final of the Glasgow Cup at the end of the previous season, and in this new campaign he had guided Rangers to a 1-0 win in the first league meeting of the season, at Ibrox. But Cup Finals are always that bit special. And this one was no different. It was a tempestuous affair. Celtic's Mo Johnston was sent off and seven other players booked after a disputed penalty seven minutes from time which gave Rangers a 2-1 win. Celtic's Tony Shepherd was also sent off – until the referee changed his mind and allowed him to carry on playing!

Rangers held on for the win and so, after only a few months in charge, Souness had brought a trophy to Ibrox. But it was the league Championship the club was after. It had been nine seasons since the title came to Ibrox. But there was now a feeling of optimism the club had not experienced since the days of Willie Waddell. Behind the scenes David Holmes was elevated to Chairman and Chief Executive following the resignation of John Paton.

In Europe, any ambitions Souness had of adding to his three winners' medals with Liverpool were dented by Borussia Mönchengladbach, who won on away goals in the third round of the UEFA Cup. In the second leg Stuart Munro and Davie Cooper were sent off by Belgian referee Alex Ponnet, which resulted in the club being fined £5,300 and full-back Munro receiving a four-match European ban for his behaviour.

The big spending continued as Souness went south again just before Christmas to bring Graham Roberts from Spurs for £450,000 and the little-known Neil Woods from Doncaster Rovers for £75,000. He also later tried to get Gary Mills from Nottingham Forest but, after terms had been agreed, the deal fell through. With the defence well bolstered and the attacking duo of Robert Fleck and Ally McCoist the most lethal in Scotland, the scene was set for a charge for the championship in the New Year.

McCoist and Fleck scored 52 league goals between them and when he scored a hat-trick against Hearts at the end of the season, McCoist surpassed Jim Forrests's post-war club record of 30 goals in a season. For his exploits, Fleck was rightly awarded the Scottish Young Player of the Year Award. He scored three hat-tricks in the league (including two against Clydebank) and in a three-day spell in September he scored hat-tricks against Tampere in the UEFA Cup and against Clydebank in the league.

There had been some changes in the backroom staff in mid-term. Don McKay left to take the manager's job at Blackburn Rovers, and Souness's former Liverpool pal Phil Boersma was brought in as trainer.

Ibrox was virtually full to its 44,000 capacity every week as the fans sensed it was to be championship year for the first time since 1978. After beating Hamilton 2-0 on 17 January, Rangers went to the top of the table for the first time during the season. The win cost them dearly as both Graham Roberts and Ian Durrant were sent off. After losing the leadership to Celtic following a goalless draw with Aberdeen in the next match, Rangers then suffered their most embarrassing moment of the season.

Souness's men were talked about as another 'treble team' but Hamilton Academical, bottom of the Premier Division all season, ended their Scottish Cup hopes when Adrian Sprott scored a 70th-minute goal at Ibrox. It also ended Chris Woods' British record of 1,196 minutes without conceding a goal.

With only the league left to concentrate on, Rangers went back to the top of the table on the last day of February after drawing 1-1 at home to Hibernian while Celtic lost 4-1 at Dundee. The Light Blues were never to lose the leadership and gradually pulled away from their deadly rivals.

The title was clinched on the penultimate Saturday of the season when one of the new recruits, Terry Butcher, scored the only goal in a 1-1 draw at Pittodrie as Celtic lost 1-2 at home to Falkirk in their first home defeat of the season. But the celebrations for the 10,000 Rangers fans at Aberdeen were marred when Souness was sent off in the 31st minute, for the second time since taking charge at Ibrox. However, Souness had been proof that Rangers needed a new broom to sweep Ibrox clean, and after the match David Holmes said of his manager; 'Without him, Rangers would still be struggling'.

At Anfield, Liverpool's success has been built on bringing in new talent only when it has fully absorbed the club's playing style – and even then only when a suitable opening occurs in the first team. Souness was to bring that philosophy to Rangers.

A club record £1.2 million was needed to bring Scottish international Richard Gough from Spurs as Souness took his expenditure past the £4 million mark. Rangers had tried to sign Gough before he went to Spurs. But the irony was that, as a youngster, Gough had spent a week on trial at Ibrox – and Rangers had not been interested in him!

Souness's former Liverpool colleague Avi Cohen cost £100,000 from

Celebrations after Rangers' victory over Celtic in the 1986 Skol Cup final. In truth it was a pretty sour occasion, fatally marred by the referee's inability to exercise effective control.

Maccabi Tel Aviv. Another ex-Spurs player, Mark Falco, came from Watford in a £300,000 deal, and former internationals Ray Wilkins and Trevor Francis were two more English faces to appear.

Before the 1987–8 season got under way, the club's annual report revealed a balance sheet loss of £1.7 million. There was a big increase in turnover but profits had been affected by a wage bill that was nearly doubled. Despite the loss David Holmes said: 'This has been one of the most exciting periods Scottish football has ever known, and for me the presence of the League Championship trophy and Skol Cup in the trophy room is a source of great pride and satisfaction'.

Rangers went into this, the second season of their brave new era, with Souness, Butcher and Roberts out of action because of suspension. They started disastrously, just as they had done 12 months earlier. A home draw with Dundee United was followed by defeats by Hibernian and Aberdeen. A McCoist hat-trick against Falkirk stopped the rot, but in the next game, the Old Firm encounter, Souness was sent off for the third time since he had taken charge at Ibrox, and Celtic won 1-0. In addition to his automatic one-match ban, Souness received a four-match suspension imposed by the Scottish FA.

In the next Old Firm match, eight weeks later, the name of Rangers hit the headlines again, and once more it was, sadly, for the wrong reasons. During the 2-2 draw at Ibrox, Chris Woods and club captain Terry Butcher were both sent off, along with Celtic's Frank McAvennie. Two weeks later Butcher, Woods, McAvennie and Graham Roberts were charged at Govan police station with conduct likely to cause a breach of the peace.

Souness may have produced a side good enough to win the league title, but its disciplinary record was no match for the team's playing skills, and the player-manager was hardly setting the best example in this area.

In 14 months 10 players had received their marching orders. On top of the prosecutions brought against their three English internationals, Rangers had internal disciplinary problems. They issued fines totalling £4,500 on Robert Fleck, reserve goalkeeper Nicky Walker, Ian Durrant, John

Graeme Souness (left) and skipper Graham Roberts pose with the Dubai Cup in December 1987 after Rangers had won the penalty shoot-out after drawing 2-2 with Everton in the final.

Hamilton's Adrian Sprott (right foreground), whose goal knocked Rangers out of the 1987 Scottish Cup in the 3rd round at Ibrox. Other players (l. to r.): Ally Brazil (Hamilton), Dave MacPherson, Graham Roberts and Robert Fleck (9).

McGregor, and an unnamed player following an incident at an Airdrie night club.

However, a week after the debacle against Celtic, the Skol Cup returned to Ibrox, and this time for keeps. After a hectic 90 minutes, which produced three goals apiece, the extra time period could still not separate the sides. A penalty shoot-out was called upon to settle a major domestic final for the first time, and Rangers won 5-3.

The Souness revolution had brought the fans swarming back to Ibrox. By the half-way stage of the season the average attendance was over 39,000. And yet, despite introducing more new players, notably the gifted winger Mark Walters from Aston Villa and striker Ian Ferguson (scorer of St Mirren's Cup-winning goal in 1987), the Rangers tempo and rhythm were too easily disrupted: their creative cohesion – as well as their individual temperaments – seemed balanced on a knife-edge. Quite often they produced a dazzling display of football only to struggle in the later stages of a match they should have won comfortably.

The club had its eye on the European Cup. This was the chance for the ultimate glory. A good 2-1 first round win over Dynamo Kiev after losing the first leg 1-0 was followed by one of the club's best performances in Europe. They were drawn against Poland's Gornik Zabrze in the second round. It was after playing Gornik in the Cup-Winners' Cup in 1969 that manager Davie White had lost his job. There was no such demise for Souness as his team played superb football – only days after the heated match against Celtic. McCoist, Durrant and Falco all scored first half goals as Rangers built a 3-1 first leg lead. A McCoist penalty in the first half of the return leg assured Rangers a place in the last eight.

However, the good run came to an abrupt halt in the quarter-final when they lost to former winners Steaua Bucharest – a side just as hard as Rangers but technically more gifted. Suddenly Rangers' season was in ruins. By then Celtic had built up a big lead in the Premier Division, and the continued story of Scottish Cup disasters had seen Dunfermline win 2-0 at East End Park in the fourth round as John Brown became the fifth Rangers player to be sent off during the season. Souness's season was made worse by the news that top scorer McCoist faced a cartilage operation and by the leg fracture in November 1987 that cost him the vital contribution of Terry Butcher. Rows between Souness and newspapermen, and a clash with defender Graham Roberts, hardly made for a placid atmosphere at Ibrox. But the manager's iron will seemed bound to bring success for the Light Blues.

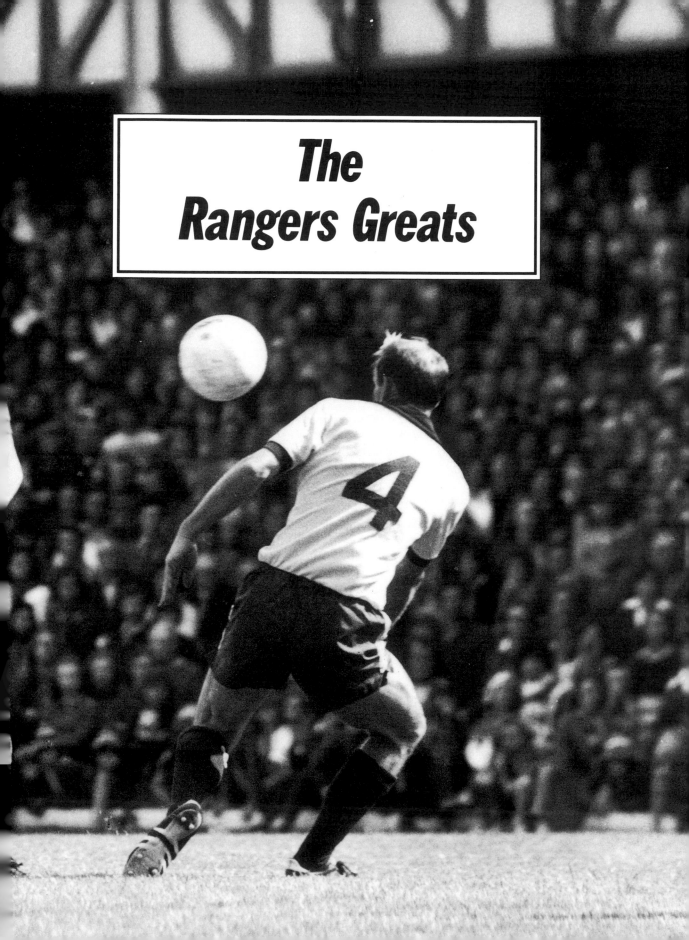

The Rangers Greats

Sammy Baird

A Stirlingshire man, born in Denny in 1930, he joined Rangers in the middle of his career, having first played for Clyde and then Preston North End. After only a year in England, Rangers brought him back across the border for £12,000 and he won a place for himself in the wing half and inside forward positions although his preference was for inside left where his height and strength – he was 5ft 11ins tall and weighed 12st 8lbs – were used to effect. Baird won championship medals with Rangers in 1956 and 1957 and played for Scotland seven times during his spell at Ibrox. His last honour was a Scottish Cup-winners' medal in the 1960 final against Kilmarnock and he was transferred to Hibernian six months later for £5,000, eventually ending his football career at Stirling Albion where he was player-manager for a short time.

Jim Baxter

Perhaps the most extravagantly gifted player ever to be seen in a Rangers jersey, his skill was comparable to that of his contemporary, George Best. Like Best he harboured a self-destructive streak and, as he confessed later, his dislike of training brought his career to a sad and premature close. A Fifer by birth, he entered senior football with Raith Rovers when he was 17 in April 1957 and the Baxter combination of arrogance and football mastery quickly attracted interest. But after several English clubs had wavered, made cautious by his frail appearance, Rangers moved in June 1960 and paid £17,500 to bring him to Ibrox where he quickly became an immense favourite. His antics were part of the attraction and even on the biggest occasion he would sit on the ball, stand on it to taunt opponents and even push it up his jersey to confuse an unwary referee.

Baxter quickly moved to the centre of the grandest stages, playing against Fiorentina in the first ever Cup-Winners' Cup final in 1961; although Rangers lost, Baxter's star was rising. In 1963 his performance in the Scotland–England match was such that the game was quickly nicknamed 'Baxter's Wembley'. He scored twice to give the Scots a 2-1 victory.

Jim Baxter

Afterwards he asserted that if Scotland had achieved a two-goal advantage during the game he would have put the ball past his own goalkeeper in order to claim a hat-trick on his first appearance at Wembley.

Honours accumulated around him as Rangers won the flag in 1961, 1963 and 1964 as well as three Scottish Cup finals in a row between 1962 and 1964. There were four Scottish League Cup medals, too, the last in 1965 when Rangers beat Celtic 2-1. Despite his disdain for authority he was made captain of Scotland for the international against Northern Ireland at Hampden Park in November 1964. But a broken ankle suffered in a European Cup-tie against Rapid Vienna was the turning point. In May 1965 he went on to Sunderland in a deal worth £72,000 and later to Nottingham Forest. Neither move was a success. Eventually he returned to Ibrox amidst banner headlines proclaiming the news 'Baxter's Back!'

The years of missed training, however, had caught up with the once skinny Fifer, who was now far from the Slim Jim of better days; he retired six months later to become a publican in Glasgow. The memory of his style and swagger remains vivid to all who saw him play. If future generations need proof of his artistry, it can be found in distilled form in the film of another Wembley encounter between England and Scotland in 1967.

England had been unbeaten since their World Cup win a year earlier, but they were given the runaround by a memorable Scottish side which included Baxter and Denis Law. Baxter's unhindered jaunt down the left wing late in the match, jersey flapping outside his shorts as he juggled the ball from one foot to another, was an exercise in disdainful superiority unlikely to be forgotten by a grateful Scottish audience.

Ralph Brand

A compact and skilful inside-left, Brand was a vital member of the Rangers side which dominated the early Sixties. Born in Edinburgh in 1936, he was a provisional signing at Ibrox in 1952 and was called up full-time two years later. He became an almost permanent fixture in the first team at the end of the decade and won the first of four championship medals in 1959, the others following in 1961, 1963 and 1964. One of his most valuable assets was an ability to score goals on important occasions, as seen in his three Scottish Cup final appearances. He netted one of Rangers' two goals in the 1962 victory over St Mirren and another in the 1-1 draw with Celtic the following year. In the replay he did even better, scoring twice as Rangers took the trophy with an emphatic 3-0 margin. In 1964 he completed a remarkable sequence by scoring the decisive third goal late in an absorbing game to give the Ibrox club a 3-1 win over an impressive Dundee side, a feat which saw Rangers complete a domestic treble of championship, League Cup and Scottish Cup. The victory against Dundee also meant that Rangers had for the third time won the Cup three times in a row.

Brand played an important role in Rangers' four League Cup wins in the 1961, 1962, 1964 and 1965 seasons, scoring against Kilmarnock in the first final and against Hearts in the replay of the second. He also appeared in Rangers' first European final, in the Cup-Winners' Cup versus Fiorentina. Eight times capped by Scotland, he moved to Manchester City in 1965 for £25,000 and won a Second Division championship medal the same season. Brand eventually became a qualified FA coach but gave up the game to be a shopkeeper and then a taxi driver in his native Edinburgh.

Terry Butcher

An inspirational early signing by Graeme Souness, Butcher was an immediate favourite at Ibrox when he was bought from Ipswich Town for £750,000 in the summer of 1986. Installed at the centre of the defence, his ability to head powerfully and accurately turned what might otherwise have been simple clearances into aerial passes. At 6ft 4ins he was an obvious focal point on the pitch and a natural choice for the role of team captain. His ability to create difficulties for opposing defences was vividly illustrated when the new-look Rangers reached for their first honour under the Souness regime. Against Celtic in the Skol Cup final Butcher moved upfield to get on the end of a corner kick with Roy Aitken and the resultant penalty kick, successfully converted by Davie Cooper, proved to be the match-winner.

The giant Englishman was similarly effective in helping Rangers win their first championship for nine years when they travelled to Pittodrie needing only a draw to take the title. Another Butcher header from a corner kick found the back of the net in a match that ended 1-1. Sadly, the following season saw him suffer badly from injuries, first when he slipped a disc early

Terry Butcher

in the season and missed England's European Championship warm-up game against West Germany, and in November when he sustained a badly broken leg in an accidental collision with Alex McLeish during a midweek league fixture with Aberdeen at Ibrox. The injury proved serious enough to keep the big man out of action for several months and Rangers' inconsistent form during that period confirmed Butcher's importance to the side.

Eric Caldow

A bedrock for Rangers and Scotland for almost a decade, he was cruelly robbed of what would surely have been an extended run of international caps when he sustained a double fracture of his left leg after only six minutes of the 1963 Wembley international between England and Scotland.

It was to be his last international match, having been Scotland's first choice at full-back for six years. Born in Ayrshire, Caldow joined Rangers in 1952. Although a slender figure in the Ibrox defence, he proved to be a resolute tackler and was notable for his ability to prompt attacks from deep-lying positions with astute passes. He won his first championship medal in

1956 and added a further four in 1957, 1959, 1961 and 1963. Caldow also won two Scottish Cup medals in 1960 and 1962 and three Scottish League Cup honours, in the 1961, 1962 and 1965 finals. During this period of prolific success he made 40 appearances for Scotland where his versatility – he could play in either full-back position – was an important asset. He moved on to Stirling Albion for a brief spell in season 1966–67. His son, also named Eric, was on the Ibrox books in the early 1980s but was not destined to repeat his father's success.

Eric Caldow

Peter Campbell

One of the earliest Rangers players to be capped, he hailed from Rhu, home of the McNeil brothers who first formed the club. A forward, he was an elegant player and was described variously as 'one of the most poetic of dribblers' and 'as graceful as a sylph'. He appeared in the Scottish Cup finals of 1877 and 1879. The first went to three games before Rangers eventually fell 3-2 to Vale of Leven and in 1879 he was denied a medal when Rangers refused to turn up for a replay against the team, claiming that they had scored a legal goal in the preceding 1-1 draw. Perhaps discouraged by this misfortune, Campbell moved on for a short period with Blackburn Rovers before becoming a seaman, a career which was cut short when he drowned in the Bay of Biscay in 1887.

Davie Cooper

An enigmatic and sometimes exasperating player, he was nevertheless blessed with gifts of great control while playing with Clydebank, from whom Rangers signed him for £100,000 in June 1977. Although he could play on either wing, Cooper preferred the left where he thrived on the service from Robert Russell and Jim Bett. He won a championship medal in his first season under Jock Wallace in 1978, although he had to wait nine years for his second when Graeme Souness restored the title to Ibrox. Cooper was a player who could rise to the big occasion and he won Scottish Cup medals in 1978, 1979 and 1981, making additional appearances in the finals in 1980, 1982 and 1983. The Scottish League Cup was also a happy hunting ground, with honours from the tournaments of 1978, 1979, 1982, 1984 and 1985.

His success continued in the Skol Cup final of 1987, in which he scored Rangers' winning goal against Celtic in their 2-1 victory. Another Skol Cup medal came the following season with the win on penalties over Aberdeen.

Because of a reluctance to give interviews he was dubbed 'Garbo' by the press, but his reticence was the product of genuine feeling that the public were not especially interested in his thoughts and off the field he proved to be a sociable and good-natured companion.

James Dawson

Known universally as Jerry, after the Jerry Dawson who kept goal for Scotland and Burnley between 1907 and 1929, Rangers' Dawson was rather younger than his namesake, being born in Falkirk in 1909. After a spell in junior football he signed for Rangers in November 1929 and won his first medal four years later when Rangers took the title in 1934. He was

goalkeeper in the championship teams of 1935, 1937 and 1939 and in that period won two Scottish Cup medals. Standing six feet tall, his virtue was reliability and a composure which was rarely ruffled. He was also able to strike his goal kicks with a sometimes dramatic spin. Dawson made 14 appearances for Scotland in the immediate pre-War years, with another seven wartime caps to add to his total. He left Rangers to move to Falkirk in 1945 and retired four years later only to return to the game for a five-year spell as manager of East Fife in the Fifties. Jerry Dawson died in January 1977.

John Drummond

One of Rangers' most highly praised players around the turn of the century, he was a defender who could fill either full-back position. He would have been the delight of most modern managers for his ability to move forward in support of his attackers although it was sometimes said that he was not so quick to chase back. He joined Rangers from Falkirk in 1892 and won three consecutive championship medals at Ibrox, in 1900, 1901 and 1902. He was also a member of four Cup-winning teams during the last years of the century and again in 1903. His fame was guaranteed when he persisted in wearing a cap during matches, the last top player to do so, in this case pleading that it kept his head cool!

Jimmy Duncanson

A Glasgow man, born in 1919, this accomplished inside forward was on Rangers' books for 12 years, although his career was interrupted by the Second World War.

Duncanson was a versatile player who could operate with ease at inside-left or on the wing. An elegant and tricky player, he was a consistent scorer with an average of nearly a goal every other game to make a total of 142 in 299 matches. He won three championship medals in 1947, 1949 and 1950 and was a member of the team which won three Scottish Cups in a row between 1948 and 1950, scoring against Clyde in the 4-1 victory of 1949. He got a goal against Aberdeen in the League Cup final of 1946 but to no avail because Rangers were beaten 3-2. However, he avenged that defeat when the same teams met in the final the following year and Duncanson scored two in a 4-0 victory. His solitary Scottish cap was awarded in 1947.

Ian Durrant

A local boy from Kinning Park, he was signed from the amateur club Glasgow United in 1984 and made a handful of first team appearances at the end of the 1984–5 season. The following league campaign saw him established as a regular in the side before his 20th birthday and he celebrated by scoring his first goal against Celtic in Rangers' 3-0 home victory in November. But he scored only one more that season, against Clydebank. However, he became an influential member of the team, playing behind the high-scoring Ally McCoist, and was instrumental in the creation of many of the striker's 33 goals in a revitalised Rangers' championship year of 1987.

The Scotland coach Andy Roxburgh was a great admirer of Durrant's talents and believed he could be a key player in Scotland's attempts to reach the World Cup finals for a fifth successive time in Italy in 1990. To that end he introduced the player to the senior squad towards the close of the unsuccessful European Championship qualifying campaign in 1987. For Durrant, there's still plenty of time.

Jimmy Fleming

Born in Glasgow in 1901, Fleming's value to Rangers was measured in kind in his transfer from St Johnstone in October 1925 when he was exchanged for three Ibrox players. He quickly established himself in the side and was a notably versatile forward capable of filling any position in the attack. However he was best equipped to lead the line and his application and skills were widely praised, in particular his ability in the air. He could be practically unstoppable on his day and scored a record-breaking nine goals against Blairgowrie in a Scottish Cup-tie in 1934. He was a member of the team which broke the supposed Cup jinx in 1928 after 25 years without success in the trophy; but although Rangers beat Celtic 4-0 in a memorable final, Fleming was not amongst the scorers. Nor was he any luckier two years later against Partick Thistle, but his endeavour was at last rewarded in another replayed final in 1932 when he scored in the Ibrox team's 3-0 victory over Kilmarnock. He won consecutive championship medals between 1927 and 1931 and added another two league honours in 1933 and 1934, moving to Ayr United the following season. He died in 1969.

Jim Forrest

Born on 22 September 1944, Forrest was a footballing prodigy whose success at schoolboy level attracted predictable attention by a battery of top clubs, but Rangers won his signature in the spring of 1960. He was then farmed out to Drumchapel Amateurs for eighteen months and returned to Ibrox to complete his apprenticeship, winning a championship medal in 1964. He was sometimes deployed as a winger but was principally a centre forward whose ability to shoot and control a ball with both feet allied with a sharp pace and the instinctive scorer's eye for a half-chance made him an Ibrox favourite. He won a Scottish Cup medal in the replayed 1966 final against Celtic which Rangers won 1-0.

However, when Rangers suffered the traumatic experience of being dumped out of the trophy by Tiny Berwick Rangers in their first defence the following season, Forrest was made a scapegoat and never played for the team again. Within two months he was transferred to Preston for £35,000. Aberdeen brought him back across the border the following year and he gained some measure of redemption in the eyes of Rangers fans when he was a member of the Dons side which beat Celtic 3-1 in the 1970 Cup final.

Tom Forsyth

A formidable, even fearsome defender whose style seemed naturally suited to commend itself to Jock Wallace during his first spell as Rangers manager. He was signed from Motherwell in October 1972 for £40,000 and added iron to midfield in a defensive role. He became known as 'Jaws' but although his movement was somewhat ungainly, and his passing ability so suspect that Alex MacDonald was instructed to play close to him and relieve him of the burden of creating attacks, he blossomed into an entirely watchable player whose career was graced by 22 international caps.

Despite, or perhaps because of, a well-publicised sarcastic remark by Tommy Docherty, then manager of Manchester United, to the effect that Forsyth was a carthorse compared to a thoroughbred in United's Martin Buchan, he developed his skills and timing considerably. He is affectionately remembered by the Scottish fans for a magnificent saving tackle on Mick Channon which almost certainly preserved Scotland's 2-1 lead over England in the 1976 international at Hampden Park.

He won three championship medals at Ibrox plus four cup honours and a League Cup medal. A rare goalscorer, he nevertheless snatched a dramatic winner in the memorable 1973 Cup final against Celtic, who were anxious to win a domestic treble during Rangers' centenary celebrations. With the score at 2-2 before an immense crowd of 122,000, a Derek Johnstone free-kick bounced off one post, rolled along the goal-line towards the other where Forsyth inelegantly but effectively bundled the ball into the net. He retired from the game, still with Rangers, in March 1982 because of a pelvic injury and, after a short spell as manager of Dunfermline, was appointed assistant to his former Ibrox colleague Tommy McLean at Motherwell in the close season of 1985.

Torrance (Torry) Gillick

Born in Airdrie in 1915, he played his schoolboy football in the Lanarkshire town before moving to the Glasgow junior club Petershill and then to

Rangers in May 1933. He could play on either wing but could claim the remarkable distinction of having been named in each of the other three positions in the old five-man attacking formation. Initially he spent only two years at Ibrox before exchanging one blue jersey for another and moving to Everton in 1935 for £8,000, then a record fee for the English club. He was a useful goalscorer at Goodison and won a League championship medal in 1939, but during the war played as a guest for Airdrie and Rangers. He returned to Ibrox in 1945 and completed a remarkable double in the Scottish Cup. He had played in the 1935 final when Rangers beat Hamilton Academical 2-1 and won another medal in the final of 1947–48 against Morton, a contest played over two games.

In the first match Morton led from the opening minute but Gillick's equaliser led to a replay before what remains a record crowd for a second game of 129,176 and this Rangers won 1-0. Gillick also won two Scottish League Cup medals with Rangers in 1947 and 1949 and moved on to Partick Thistle two years later for a single season. He died in December 1971.

Douglas Gray

Born in the north-east of Scotland in the Aberdeenshire town of Alford, he joined Rangers, his first and only senior club, soon after his 20th birthday in 1925. He was to prove an unshakeable asset in a career which lasted more than two decades. At a mere 5ft 7½ins and weighing in at around 11 stone he hardly seemed to have the physique for a protracted spell at right-back but in fact Dougie Gray made 801 appearances in the League and Cup for Rangers, a total which remains the club record and his 879 appearances in all is a Scottish record.

He was a cornerstone of the immense and intimidating Ibrox presence built by manager Willie Struth and won an astonishing ten championship medals along with six Scottish Cup honours, all before the Second World War. What the total might have been but for the War is anybody's guess. His last appearance came in October 1945 although Rangers registered him as a player for another eighteen months, perhaps in the belief that he was indeed indestructible.

His remarkable consistency was possible because of his relative immunity to injuries and this in turn appears to have stemmed from his small build and the need to protect himself from damage through acute timing. He would almost certainly have fitted easily into the modern game with his preference for creative clearances on the ground. He died in 1972.

John Greig

The man who, more than any other player in Rangers' history, exemplifies the club's stature in Scottish football. Ironically, Greig was born in Edinburgh and was a confirmed Hearts supporter, even playing his early football with an amateur club called Edina Hearts. He joined the Ibrox staff in August 1960 and his playing career of 18 years brought him 857 senior appearances. If his playing role had not been sensationally ended by the unexpected resignation of Jock Wallace as manager in May 1978, which saw Greig appointed as his successor, he would in all probability have appeared in the 23 games which would have broken Dougie Gray's record. As it was he accumulated a fine medal collection as a vital part of the championship teams of 1963, 1964, 1975, 1976 and 1978. He laid his hands on the Scottish

John Greig

Cup six times and the League Cup on four occasions.

The qualities of leadership which made him an obvious choice as Rangers' captain also made him an inspirational force for Scotland, for whom he made 44 appearances. He was twice named Scottish Player of the Year, in 1966 and 1976 and also took part in two European Cup-Winners' Cup finals, against Bayern Munich in 1967 when Rangers were beaten 1-0 in Nuremberg after extra time and in May 1972 when the club won its first European trophy by beating Moscow Dynamo 3-2.

He came to Rangers as inside-forward but eventually settled into a habitual role as left-half. When his career is assessed by future historians of the game they would do well to consider that John Greig's career was played in the shadow of a certain amount of misfortune. He was club captain throughout the trying period when Celtic won nine championships in a row under the presiding genius of Jock Stein, and when the horrific Ibrox disaster occurred on 2 January 1971.

At what should have been the crowning moment of his playing days, as Rangers won the European Cup-Winners' Cup, he was presented with the trophy in an underground room at the Nou Camp Stadium in Barcelona after a harmless pitch invasion by Scottish supporters had been turned into a riot by the clumsy intervention of the Spanish police. His unforeseen elevation to the position of Rangers' manager deprived him of the chance of an apprenticeship at some less demanding club and although his managerial record of five consecutive Scottish Cup finals and four League Cup finals would have satisfied virtually any other club, the lack of a league title led to his resignation in October 1984. He did, however, entirely deserve his newspaper nickname of 'Mr Rangers' and was awarded a merited MBE in the Queen's Jubilee Honours List of 1977.

Willie Henderson

A diminutive, myopic winger, he was added to the Ibrox staff in August 1960 at the same time as Greig. He was another precocious talent and a measure of his effectiveness can be gauged from the fact that he deposed Rangers' dynamic and forceful resident at outside-right, Alex Scott, who moved on to Everton in 1963 for £39,000.

Henderson, known familiarly to the Ibrox following as Wee Wullie, deserved his nickname, standing as he did a mere 5ft 4½ins tall. But his lack of inches were not a handicap and he had the beating of almost every full back he encountered. His ball control was lavishly entertaining and despite his opponents' efforts to contain him against the touchline, he would repeatedly beat them on the outside. After acquiring a respectable collection of honours with Rangers he travelled south for a brief and uneventful spell with Sheffield Wednesday before moving on to Hong Kong Rangers for three years which saw him captain the Hong Kong national side.

His short-sightedness was famous and during one intense Rangers–Celtic match he unwittingly enquired of the Celtic bench how much time remained in the contest. Celtic manager Jock Stein entered into the spirit of the moment and obliged with an answer to which Henderson, still unaware of his error, replied: 'Thanks, boss . . .' to the vast amusement of the opposing dugout.

Colin Jackson

He was born in Falkirk but played his juvenile football adjacent to Glasgow with Rutherglen Schools before signing for Rangers in 1962. He was farmed out to the Aberdeen amateur club Sunnybank before returning to Ibrox on a permanent basis in October 1963. Jackson began his career as a left half but when he eventually earned himself a permanent place in the first team he found the berth occupied by John Greig and so moved to centre half. It was a position he occupied comfortably and in which his height, a little over 6ft, served him well.

He was known as 'Bomber' to his teammates but was hardly a flash character and his quiet manner off the field was reflected in his calm and effective style as a player. He made eight appearances for Scotland in 1975 and 1976, played in a title-winning Rangers team three times with the same number of Scottish Cup medals and four League Cup honours. He should and would have had a Cup-Winners' Cup medal in 1972 but injury prevented him from playing in the final against Moscow Dynamo and his place was taken by the youthful Derek Johnstone. He was on Norton's books for a month in 1982 and moved on for a short spell with Partick Thistle before quitting the game to go into partnership in an East Kilbride printing firm.

William Jardine

Despite his Christian name, this long-serving and versatile player was known to one and all as Sandy because of his light hair. Another of Rangers' Edinburgh imports, he was born in the capital on Hogmanay, 1948 and after being signed as a schoolboy in 1963 became a full-time player in December 1965. A rangy, athletic individual, he began his playing career as a forward and indeed featured in an attacking role in the Cup-Winners' Cup final of

1967 when Rangers lost 1-0 to Bayern Munich. His natural role was in midfield or at full-back and he was recognised as a world class player when he played in Scotland's three World Cup finals matches of 1974 as part of a 38-cap sequence which also took him to Argentina. A durable presence at Ibrox, he won 16 domestic honours in all three competitions as well as a Cup-Winners' Cup medal against Moscow Dynamo.

His total of appearances for Rangers is also formidable and numbers 773 with 93 goals to his credit. When he left Ibrox in 1982 it was to become assistant manager to his Rangers colleague Alex MacDonald at Hearts, a couple of hundred yards from his former school. Remarkably Jardine went on to pass 1,000 appearances in first class matches, the only Scottish player to do so and was a key element in Hearts' heroic but ultimately unsuccessful quest for the Cup and league double in 1985-6. He was named Player of the Year by the Scottish Football Writers in 1986 and retained a special place in the affections of Rangers fans until he retired in the autumn of 1987.

Willie Johnston

Although born in Glasgow in 1946, Johnston was a Fifer in speech and indeed played his initial football with the miners' team Lochore Welfare until Rangers called him up in 1964. He was rechristened Bud by his teammates and Ibrox fans, who loved his close control and acceleration along the left flank where few defenders could catch him on the turn. He consistently delivered fine crosses and won 22 Scottish caps. In his two spells with Rangers he picked up two Scottish Cup medals and two League Cup medals, which seemed a poor reward for his talents, but he passed a lengthy spell with West Bromwich Albion during the Seventies when Rangers won a series of championships. After Albion he went to Vancouver Whitecaps to play in the North American Soccer League before returning to Ibrox.

He was a volatile personality, quick to erupt in the face of provocation and was sent off for the 13th time in a match against Aberdeen, in his second Ibrox tenure in 1980. He achieved worldwide notoriety for the incident in 1978 when he was sent home from Scotland's ill-fated World Cup trip to Argentina after failing a dope test.

But for all his faults, he was a crowd-pleaser and a favourite with the Rangers' support.

Derek Johnstone

A Dundonian by birth, he guaranteed himself a place in football history when at 16 he became the youngest player to appear in a major British cup final on 24 October 1970. Johnstone doubled his distinction when he scored the only goal of the game for Rangers, who were not favourites to beat Celtic in the Scottish League Cup final. Fittingly the score came from a header because it was in the air that Johnstone's greatest asset was to be found. Although he played most of his early professional football in the striker's position, he was a confident performer at centre-back where he appeared for Rangers in the 1972 Cup Winners' Cup final in place of the injured Colin Jackson.

He was nominated Player of the Year in 1978 but, despite thrilling goals against Northern Ireland and Wales in the home championships, he was not part of Ally McLeod's plans in Argentina and did not add to his eventual total of 14 international appearances there.

Stewart Kennedy

Born in Stirling, this tall, athletic goalkeeper made his way to Rangers by way of Dunfermline Athletic and an unusual step down to junior football with Linlithgow Rose before moving back to the senior grade with Stenhousemuir where he was spotted by Jock Wallace. Rangers paid £10,000 for his services in April 1973 and Kennedy stayed seven years at Ibrox during which time he won two championship medals, in 1975 and 1978. In 1975 he won three of his five caps for Scotland in the home championship series but suffered the misfortune of playing in an embarrassing 5-1 defeat by England at Wembley. Although by no means to blame for all of the goals, the stigma remained with him and he played no more international matches. Wallace, however, remained faithful to his protege and Kennedy was able to add a League Cup medal to his title honours in 1978. Two years later he moved on to Forfar Athletic and an extended tenure at Station Park.

Peter McCloy

An immense goalkeeper at 6ft 4ins and weighing 14st 3lbs, McCloy won four international caps. He joined Rangers in March 1970 in a player exchange deal with Motherwell and has retained his connection with the club as a member of the coaching staff under Graeme Souness. He played at Ibrox throughout the Seventies, alternating in lengthy spells with Stewart Kennedy and both goalkeepers were able to claim championship medals in 1975 and 1978. McCloy played in victorious Rangers teams in four Scottish Cup finals and four League Cup finals and was in goal for the Cup-Winners' Cup victory in Barcelona.

Nicknamed the Girvan Lighthouse in reference to his birthplace on the Ayrshire coast, McCloy was an equally proficient golfer and has played for Scotland at amateur level.

Preceding pages *Rangers line up after clinching the 1986–7 Premier League championship in the match against St Mirren in May 1987.*

Ally McCoist

A prolific striker who attracted attention when he moved from Lanarkshire schoolboy football to St Johnstone in 1978, McCoist was soon a target for Rangers manager John Greig. Despite offers from Ibrox he chose to move south of the border to Sunderland, who paid £350,000 for him in 1981. But after a frustrating spell he returned to Scotland in a £185,000 deal in June 1983.

Eighteen goals in the league and League Cup marked his first season at Ibrox and he was easily the top scorer in Rangers' championship season of 1986–87 under Graeme Souness. Brave and eager, sharp near goal though with a tendency to snap at the ball when anxious, he has nevertheless shown that he is capable of improving his game and deservedly brought himself to the attention of Scotland coach Andy Roxburgh in 1987.

Ally McCoist

John McColl

Better known as Ian McColl, this elegant and creative wing-half was the grandson of William McColl, centre half of Renton towards the end of the last century. Like his grandfather he was born in Alexandria and made an early impression in schools football. A player who had a thoughtful look about him, he had the credentials to prove that his brains were not confined to his feet, having graduated with a B.Sc. degree from Glasgow University. He joined Rangers as a professional from Queen's Park just before the end of World War II and won the first of six championship medals with the team two years later. His last league honour came a decade later and he also enjoyed success in five Scottish Cups and four League Cup finals before retiring in the close season of 1961. In November 1960, before the end of his playing career he was appointed manager of Scotland, a post he held until

May 1965, when he was succeeded by Jock Stein, and he went on to manage Sunderland for two and a half years. McColl won 14 Scotland caps.

Alex MacDonald

A Glasgow man, born there in March 1948, he personified the fighting bantam image of the city. He usually operated on what would now be termed the left side of midfield but in the late Sixties that meant that he shuttled between inside-forward and wing-half. St Johnstone brought him into senior football in 1966 after having him on the books for nine months. Two years later he was transferred to Ibrox for £50,000 where his relentless energy and application were greatly appreciated. He played an important role in the successful Rangers side moulded by Jock Wallace in the early Seventies and he accumulated a fine harvest of medals during his time with the Light Blues. Along with Sandy Jardine he moved to Hearts and combined his duties with an extended playing career which saw him warmly received on visits to Ibrox. He won the Scottish Manager of the Year award in 1986.

Ron McKinnon

A fixture at Ibrox throughout the Sixties, McKinnon had an unusual start in football. He played first for the Glasgow junior club Benburb as an outside left but was thought to be too small or perhaps too frail for the physical demands of the junior game. However he moved on to Dunipace and stepped back to left half at which point he suddenly sprouted the necessary inches to give him command of the air. Rangers were alerted to his new and successful role as a centre half and in the summer of 1959 he moved to Ibrox where Scot Symon was assembling a team of considerable talents. He was pivot in a fine half-back line which consisted of Greig, McKinnon and Baxter and earned himself two championship, four Scottish Cup and three League Cup medals before retiring in 1973 and moving on to South Africa and Australia. His twin brother Donnie played at the same time with Partick Thistle.

Tommy McLean

The most junior of three brothers who all made a name in football management, Tommy McLean was born in Lanarkshire in 1947 and was signed by Kilmarnock at the age of 15 after showing early promise which won him three Scottish amateur international caps. He won a championship medal with Kilmarnock while only 18. The then Kilmarnock manager Willie Waddell was an open admirer of McLean's play and when Waddell took over as Rangers' manager in succession to Davie White, he brought him to Ibrox in 1971 for £70,000.

A diminutive player at 5ft 4ins, McLean was not a particularly speedy winger on his favoured right flank but his ability to hit menacing and accurate long passes as well as a good positional sense more than compensated. He also had a gift for placing a dead ball exactly where he intended it to fall. This was the source of many goals for the likes of Derek Johnstone, for example, and one particularly memorable pass in Rangers' 3-2 away victory over PSV Eindhoven in the European Cup in 1978 led to the

Preceding pages *Richard
Gough turns away after scoring a
late equaliser in the draw against
Celtic in October 1987. Gough,
one of the classiest defenders in
Britain, returned to Scotland in
1987 after a successful spell with
Tottenham.*

winning goal for the Scottish champions. He won a Cup-Winners' Cup
medal in 1972 along with three title honours and two from successful League
Cup finals. He became assistant Rangers manager under John Greig and
went on to become manager of Motherwell, a job previously held by his
older brother Willie. The third McLean brother is, of course, Jim whose
name will always be associated with Dundee United.

John McMillan

Known universally as Ian McMillan, his nickname at Ibrox was The Wee
Prime Minister, a reference to the Premier of the time, Harold Macmillan. An
Airdrie man who signed for the town team in 1948, he joined Rangers at the
comparatively late age of 27 ten years later. An inside forward of great guile,
his class was reminiscent of Jimmy Mason of Third Lanark. His ability to
find attackers with telling passes contributed greatly to Rangers' championships of 1959, 1961 and 1963 and three Scottish Cup successes in 1960, 1962
and 1963. He earned two League Cup medals in 1961 and 1962 before
returning to Airdrie for a fee of £5,000 and he retired from football with an
aggravated injury three years later.

Moses McNeil

One of the McNeil brothers from Rhu who founded Rangers, he provided
the main drive behind the club in its vulnerable early years, although he did
shift across Glasgow for a few months with Queen's Park. His energy
appears to have translated itself on to the football field where he was
reported to be 'too much addicted to charging'. But he was also a good
dribbler and was noted for his ability to deliver a telling long-distance pass.
He won two Scottish caps but his place in football history is guaranteed, of
course, by his part in the formation of Rangers.

Bob McPhail

One of Rangers' great players between the Wars, he had already won a
Scottish Cup medal with Airdrie before he began a run of success which saw
him accumulate nine championship medals and six Scottish Cup prizes with
the Rangers team which dominated the late Twenties and most of the
Thirties.

A forceful inside left, he played alongside the legendary Hughie Gallacher
at Airdrie and was capable of scoring useful goals, a habit he carried on at
Ibrox where he netted 281 in 466 outings. He would have been regarded as a
successful ball-winner in midfield nowadays and his shooting ability,
which was widely regarded during his heyday, would have been a
particular asset in the modern game. McPhail won 17 Scottish caps and
retired as a player after a brief Wartime spell with St Mirren, but he was a
familiar figure at Ibrox right through to the Graeme Souness era.

Bob McPhail

Davie Meiklejohn

Once described by Bob McPhail as 'the most complete footballer I ever saw',
he was a man who took his football earnestly and became one of the most

stalwart players the Scottish game has seen. He joined Rangers in 1919 from Maryhill Juniors and stayed at Ibrox for the rest of his playing career. Not especially tall at 5ft 10ins, he made up for the want of a couple of inches with an impressive resolution which was directed as much at his teammates as the opposition. Inevitably, he became captain and although he could and did play at wing-half, his best position was at centre half.

His positional sense was astute and he had immense stamina and strength. Thirteen championship medals were his reward. He took a successful penalty in the Cup final of 1928 which led to a 4-0 victory over Celtic and broke Rangers' 25-year run without a win in the final of the tournament. They won another four with Meiklejohn in their ranks. He became manager of Partick Thistle in 1947 and remained at Firhill until his death in 1959. Those who saw him play are apt to contend that he was Rangers' greatest centre half.

Jimmy Millar

An Edinburgh man, born in 1934, he joined Rangers in 1955 for a fee of £5,000 and stayed for 12 years which brought many honours to the club. A natural goalscorer, he was versatile and could adapt easily to other positions. He played frequently as an inside-forward and wing-half. His ball control was a particular strength along with considerable stamina. Millar won three championship medals and was an important figure in five Scottish Cup triumphs, scoring both goals in the 2-0 win over Kilmarnock in 1960 and another two in the 3-1 defeat of Dundee in 1964.

Alan Morton

Known universally as the Wee Blue Devil after his devastating display when Scotland's Wembley Wizards annihilated England 5-1, Alan Morton was the archetype of the Scottish outside left and arguably the greatest winger ever to come out of Britain. Every reliable witness who watched him play or who appeared on the same field testified to his innate ability and immense skills. He was certainly not a physical giant, being only 5ft 4ins tall, but his gifts were prodigious. He was well-proportioned and possessed strong legs; he was devastatingly fast, with brilliant ball control. His low centre of gravity allowed him to turn inside opponents without warning and he could strike a cross with uncanny accuracy. As if this were not enough, he was apt to score goals from positions which would have defied a Brazilian. He will never be forgotten by the crowds who saw him in action against Third Lanark when he beat the great Jimmy Brownlie, and against Celtic when he left six defenders flat-footed for a sensational drive. One of Morton's trademarks was a turn on the bye line which ended with the ball being flighted to the far post for some waiting colleague to head in on goal.

Alan Morton

He played his first senior football with the amateurs of Queen's Park but Rangers moved for him in 1920 and he began an association with the club which lasted almost until his death in 1971. He was not a player to whom all good things came naturally and although he could use both feet well, he had worked hard as a schoolboy to bring the left up to the same standard as the right.

He played in 495 games, scored 115 goals and won a total of 92 caps and medals. The striking portrait which hangs inside the marble entrance hall at Ibrox signifies his stature in the club's history. His Scotland career is forever

immortalised in the memory of the 1928 Wembley match when his trickery and pin-point passes laid on three goals for Alex Jackson.

Graham Roberts

Part of the Souness breed of Ibrox players, he arrived from Spurs in December 1986 for a fee of £450,000 and became the fifth Englishman to be signed by Rangers from a Football League club inside six months, a Scottish record. With six English caps to his credit he was a solid, uncompromising defender who slotted in immediately beside Terry Butcher. He was blooded in an Old Firm derby within a couple of weeks of his arrival when Rangers won 2-0 and began the erosion of Celtic's substantial points lead which ended in the championship.

In recognition of his powers of inspiration, he was appointed club captain after Terry Butcher broke his leg in November 1987, a position he kept for the rest of the season.

Alex Scott

A Falkirk boy who played his juvenile and adolescent football in that area, he was signed provisionally by Rangers in 1954 and called up professionally the following year. He spent eight years at Ibrox where he occupied the

Alex Scott

96

outside right berth and his splendid acceleration and ability to swerve inside a covering defender to deliver a fierce shot was a striking feature of the team's play during the four successful championship campaigns in which he took part between 1956 and 1961. Scott also won a Scottish Cup medal in 1960 when Rangers beat Kilmarnock 2-0 and when the Ayrshire side were beaten by the same score in the League Cup final of 1960–61, he scored the decisive second goal. He moved on to Everton in February 1963 and continued his success at Goodison where he was part of the title-winning team the same year and added a Cup medal in 1966.

Bobby Shearer

Another in the inspirational line of Ibrox skippers, he was born in Hamilton in 1931 and played for the Academicals for five years in which he filled every position except goalkeeper. Perhaps attracted by his versatility, Rangers paid £2,000 for him in 1955 and certainly got their money's worth. He was a natural leader and his drive at right back helped Rangers win six championships between 1956 and 1964, as well as three Scottish Cup victories and a League Cup triple. He was able to claim a somewhat unfortunate distinction in football management after he left Rangers. Having taken over at another Glasgow club, Third Lanark, in January 1967, he was not to complete a full term at Cathkin because the club folded the following close season, the last Scottish senior team to go out of business.

Dave Smith

A vital link in the Rangers team which won the Cup-Winners' Cup, he was a left-half who could perform as a sweeper if the occasion demanded. Aberdeen born, he was on the Dons' books for five years before Rangers moved for him in 1966 in a deal worth £40,000. Unfortunately he joined the club at a time which coincided with Celtic's great years under Jock Stein and his sole honour came in the victory over Moscow Dynamo. However, he was a gifted and above all elegant performer who could strike an accurate ball with economy and was well able to position himself shrewdly to obstruct opposing attacks. He had a chequered career after leaving Ibrox, moving to Arbroath, Berwick Rangers, Los Angeles Aztecs and South Africa. His brother was Dundee United's Doug Smith.

Graeme Souness

When he was appointed player-manager at Rangers in April 1986, the British football world was as astonished as the Ibrox support, particularly because Souness had no previous connection with the club or the city. Born in the capital, he played his boyhood football for Edinburgh Schools and although Rangers were interested, Spurs moved first to secure his services. After a year as an apprentice at White Hart Lane he became a professional, moving to Middlesborough three years later and on to Liverpool in 1978 where he won five championship medals and three European Cup honours as well as playing in four League Cup teams. It was this success which moved Rangers' chief executive David Holmes to approach Souness in Italy where he was playing for Sampdoria in Genoa. His arrival was sensational and his debut no less so when he was sent off after barely half-an-hour of his playing

Graeme Souness at a training session in July 1986.

debit in the Scottish League against Hibernian at Easter Road in August 1986. He was to be dismissed again the following May in the 1-1 draw with Aberdeen which saw Rangers win their first league title in eight years. He continued to play for the club in the studied midfield role which had seen him dictate many a vital game for Liverpool and Scotland, and he guided Rangers to a European Cup quarter final against Steaua Bucharest in March 1988. But with several of his most recent signings injured or ineligible, the Light Blues were denied an appearance in the last four by a slim 3-2 aggregate defeat.

Colin Stein

Made history when he joined Rangers from Hibernian in October 1968 for £100,000, the first six-figure deal between Scottish clubs. Mainly a centre-forward although he could move inside if required, he was a traditional striker with good balance and was brave in his head-on attacks on opposing defences. But like several other players whose talent would probably have been rewarded by honours, he joined Rangers at a time when success was elusive and medals from the 1972 Cup-Winners' Cup and the League Cup of 1971 made up his total at Ibrox. He was, however, recognised by Scotland and made 21 appearances in the dark blue jersey. He moved to Coventry City in October 1972 but returned for another sojourn with Rangers between 1975 and 1977, although he was not a regular feature in the first team.

Colin Stein

Willie Thornton

Born in the West Lothian village of Winchburgh in 1920, he certainly qualified as a precocious talent. He joined Rangers as an amateur in March 1936 and a year later was signed as a professional. His league debut came at the tender age of 16.

Three years later he won his first championship medal and his scoring ability as a centre-forward (sometimes inside-forward) was of great importance to Rangers' success. His particular skill was heading and he would surely have won many more honours but for the Second World War. As it was, he distinguished himself in the conflict and was awarded the Military Medal. He later resumed his career with Rangers and was a member of a further three title-winning teams between 1947 and 1950 with three Scottish Cup successes during the same period, which also saw Rangers win the League Cup twice. He played for his country on seven occasions and was honoured as Scottish Player of the Year in 1952.

Willie Thornton

Thomas Vallance

Another of Rangers' founders, he was a devoted and consistent left-back who looked gangly at 6ft 1½ins but who possessed a deceptive strength which overcame many a bulkier-looking opponent. He played at left back and was team captain for nine years before leaving for Assam, where the climate disagreed with him; he returned to play in charity matches. He became Rangers' president in 1883 and held the post for six years. These distinctions were only part of his claim to fame because he also set a Scottish long-jump record which lasted for 14 years, and two of his paintings were hung in the Royal Scottish Academy, making him one of the few players who could truly prove himself to have been an artist.

Willie Waddell

A right-winger with the build of a centre-forward, Waddell hailed from the village of Forth in Lanarkshire where he was born in 1921. But like many another player, he found that what might have been his most productive football years were interrupted by the War. His power was not the only ingredient in his success. He possessed good close control and change of pace which often deceived opposing full backs and allowed Waddell to launch crosses which were often converted into goals by Willie Thornton, who was the first to acknowledge his colleague's contribution.

He won 27 caps (ten of them awarded during wartime) and collected eight championship, cup and League Cup medals during his spell at Ibrox, which encompassed 558 matches and 143 goals. He went on to manage Kilmarnock to a title success and returned to Ibrox as manager in 1969. He later became general manager and a director.

Willie Waddell (right) trains at Ibrox with Willie Woodburn.

Davie Wilson

A native of Glasgow, his first professional club was Rangers in May 1956 and with his white-blond hair he was a distinctive outside left and occasionally inside left. He was a winger blessed with close control who could produce a decided turn of speed and was not easily intimidated by physical full-backs. In the words of the Ibrox support 'he played for the jersey', a term of particular praise. He was also a useful scorer who could hit the heights on his day, scoring a double hat-trick against Falkirk in 1962. He made 22 appearances for Scotland and continued his club career with Dundee United in 1967 after accumulating 13 medals at Ibrox.

Willie Woodburn

A player with a very strong claim to be Rangers' finest centre-half, a distinction which might have to be shared with George Young, who played alongside Woodburn in the Light Blues' famous Iron Curtain defence of the late Forties and early Fifties. Woodburn was not a huge centre-half at 5ft 11½ins and 12st 1lb but was an obvious attraction for Rangers when they signed him from the amateur club Ashton Juveniles. His best period followed the War and he won 24 Scottish caps and ten medals from the three domestic tournaments. However, his character had a distinctly abrasive streak which caused him to be ordered off five times and although this total is hardly exceptional by modern standards, the Scottish Football Association thought it reprehensible enough to ban him *sine die* in September 1954. Woodburn and Rangers parted company the following year and although the ban was subsequently lifted, Woodburn thought it not worth his while to resume playing at the age of 37 – an anti-climactic end to a distinguished career.

Willie Woodburn (right) at the heart of Rangers defence.

George Young

A burly, indeed massive, component of Rangers' 'Iron Curtain' defence, here was a man whose tackles were of the boneshaking variety. Young played out of his natural position of centre-half to accommodate Willie Woodburn in that berth and possessed an immense kick that could change the direction of play with a single swing at the ball. He helped guide Rangers to half a dozen post-War championships and was a natural Scotland captain who established a record of 53 caps, including 48 appearances as skipper. He was a target for critics who disliked the scale of his punts, but those who played with him gave him detailed credit for having used a shrewd tactical brain and insist that he was a capable passer along the deck. He was a wholehearted player whose devotion to club and country was taken for granted. He was nicknamed Corky because he carried a lucky charm in the form of the cork from the first champagne bottle to be opened at the celebration banquet which followed Rangers' Scottish Cup win in 1948.

Unforgettable Matches

Scottish Cup Final, 1909 (2nd Match)

Rangers 1 *(Gordon)* **Celtic 1** *(Quinn)*

On 10 April 1909 Rangers and Celtic fought out a great Scottish Cup final, drawing 2-2. Seven days later they were involved in a replay that was to have one of the most shameful conclusions in Scottish Cup history.

In between the two matches, Celtic had suggested to the Scottish FA that extra time should be played if the replay ended all square. Rangers were against the idea, which never went before the full SFA committee. Celtic's suggestion received widespread publicity but the outcome did *not*, and many fans, and indeed players, thought extra time would be played if required.

Celtic had dominated the first game and were favourites to win the trophy for the third successive year and thus emulate the feat of the great Queen's Park and Vale of Leven sides. Rangers made several changes for the second game, notably with the introduction of goalscoring centre-forward Reid, a recent signing from Portsmouth.

The game was played in a blustery wind and, considering the clubs were the top two in Scotland, they mustered little enthusiasm. Rangers struck first in the 20th minute when Gordon scored from a great solo effort. Reid nearly made sure of the trophy in the first minute of the second half after his shot was fumbled by Adams, but the 'keeper recovered to retrieve the ball.

After 18 minutes of th second half, however, Celtic equalised from a corner. Celtic had the better of the play in the second half despite playing into the wind and they came close to victory from another corner.

As the final whistle blew, with the scores level, the confusion arose.

Many fans believed extra time was to be played. The fact that seven players stayed on the field added fuel to their belief. But there was to be no more play. Thousands of fans spilled onto the pitch and a wholesale riot broke out. Goal posts and nets were set on fire, as were pay boxes and parts of the ground. Fans and police were involved in a pitch battle and the fighting went on until seven o'clock in the evening. Miraculously nobody was killed but nearly one hundred were injured.

At a Scottish FA inquiry it was at first suggested a third match should take place. But both clubs were united in their appeal to the SFA to withhold the cup in fear of further violence. The SFA agreed and so, for the one and only time in British soccer history, a major trophy was withheld.

Teams: *Rangers:* Rennie, Law, Craig, Gordon, Stark, Galt, Bennett, MacDonald, Reid, McPherson, Smith.
Celtic: Adams, McNair, Weir, Young, Dodds, Hay, Kivlichan, McMenemy, Quinn, Somers, Hamilton.

Scottish Cup Final, 1928

Rangers 4 *(Meiklejohn (pen), McPhail, Archibald 2)* **Celtic 0**

Rangers had not won the Scottish Cup in 25 years. Since beating Hearts to win the trophy in 1903, they had appeared in five finals and lost the lot. On

the other hand, Celtic had won the trophy nine times in that period. Rangers had one of the best line-ups in the club's history. They just *had* to win the trophy to end the music hall jokes about their inability to lift the famous 'tin pot'.

The 22 men who took the field in front of a 100,00-plus Hampden crowd were a cornucopia of talent. The only uncapped player in the Rangers team was full-back Hamilton, while only Donoghue, McFarlane and Connelly of Celtic had not won full international honours. Rangers headed the league and Celtic were second at the time of the final. So the scene was set for one of the great Cup Finals.

As often happens at Hampden, there was a strong swirling wind. Celtic won the toss and had the wind behind them in the first half. With such an advantage, and with Rangers having the disadvantage of a hoodoo to overcome, it was widely expected the Parkhead team would build up a comfortable first half lead. But, surprisingly, there were no goals in the opening 45 minutes.

Celtic were not only poor in front of goal but gave the ball away a great deal, and allowed Rangers to take control. Morton and Archibald opened up the Celtic defence time and time again. By the end of the first half the large crowd were amazed that it was Rangers who had not scored, despite playing into the wind.

The second half was only ten minutes old when Cunningham started a Rangers move and got the ball to Fleming. He beat off a Jimmy McStay tackle and shot. It beat 'keeper Thomson and was clearly a foot over the line when Celtic skipper Willie McStay scooped the ball out of the goal. Referee Willie Bell gave a penalty despite the Rangers' protests that it was over the line.

A big responsibility fell upon the shoulders of the penalty-taker. Captain Meiklejohn could not ask any of his team-mates to shoulder such a burden. So up stepped the skipper for one of the most important spot kicks in the club's history. He looked calm as he placed the ball on the spot. He looked calm as he ran up for the kick. And he calmly put the ball into the net. After the match Meiklejohn admitted he had been shaking like a leaf, and continued to do so for ten minutes after converting the kick!

Rangers showed complete mastery from that point as Celtic wilted. Rangers, however, were determined to build on their slender lead.

After 65 minutes Rangers were awarded yet another of their many corners. Archibald placed the ball beautifully on to the foot of master goalscorer McPhail who rammed home number two. The Cup jinx was now well and truly out of the way. It was just a matter of how many more Rangers would score.

Two minutes later Archibald scored the first of two of the finest goals seen at Hampden.

He took a long pass from Craig and broke away on his own before hitting a shot on the run into the corner of the net. As the fans were still talking about that goal, he scored one even better. This time he hit a shot from 30 yards out. Goalkeeper Thomson had a clear sight of the ball but was powerless to stop it.

Rangers could have had even more goals as Cunningham, Morton and Fleming all came close in the last ten minutes. But the goal tally was to stand at four, without reply.

The Light Blues gave a dazzling display of football, and the two goals from Archibald stand out as the highlights of a great game.

It had been said that Rangers had beaten themselves in the cup over the previous 25 years. But the eleven men who pulled on the blue shirts this day had the desire and the will to end the Scottish Cup bogy. They certainly did that, and in fine style. The win was to herald the start of the greatest era in the club's history. The period leading up to the outbreak of the War became known as the 'Eleven Great Years' of Glasgow Rangers.

Teams: *Rangers:* T. Hamilton, Gray, R. Hamilton, Buchanan, Meiklejohn, Craig, Archibald, Cunningham, Fleming, McPhail, Morton.
Celtic: J. Thomson, W. McStay, Donoghue, Wilson, J. McStay, McFarlane, Connolly, A. Thompson, McGrory, McInally, McLean.

Moscow Dynamo, 1945

Rangers 2 *(Smith, Young (pen))* **Moscow Dynamo 2** *(Kartsev 2)*

On the Wednesday afternoon of 28 November 1945 it seemed as if the whole of Glasgow wanted to pack into Ibrox for the visit of the crack Russian team Moscow Dynamo. The following day, the excuses used by employees to their bosses as to why they were not in work would most probably have made a humorous book of its own. If they were all true then the Glasgow cemeteries would have been crammed tight with 'dead grandmothers. . .'

Dynamo had come north of the border for the fourth and final match of their British tour. Having been held by Chelsea, they then thrashed Cardiff City 10-1 and beat Arsenal, who included the two Stanleys, Matthews and Mortensen, in their ranks. Could Rangers do what their English and Welsh counterparts could not do, and beat the Russians?

Dynamo surprised the 90,000 all-ticket crowd by coming out for a full 15 minute kick-in before the match. And once play got under way at 2.15 they gave a display of great passing, speed and fitness. The Russians opened the scoring as early as the second minute when inside forward Kartsev hammered home a free kick from 20 yards. Rangers had a chance to equalise five minutes later when Billy Williamson was brought down in the box but

*Incident in the Rangers'
goalmouth during the 1945 match
against Moscow Dynamo.*

Waddell's spot kick was deflected on to the bar and to safety by 'keeper Khomich. The Dynamo goalkeeper thrilled the Ibrox fans with his acrobatic displays throughout the match.

But with their chance missed, Rangers succumbed to the Dynamo pressure, and in particular from the fast moving wing halves Blinkov and Oreshkin. They complemented their forwards when an attack was building but if possession was lost, they were quick to get back in defence to help out.

A great passing move involving all five Moscow forwards resulted in their second goal after 24 minutes. It was Kartsev who added the final touches to a great move as he gave Dawson little chance.

One minute later, however, Rangers reduced the arrears. Shaw punted the ball upfield. It was knocked on to Smith and in a rather scrambled effort he managed to lob the ball over Khomich. In scoring, Smith collided with the 'keeper and injured his leg.

In the second period Rangers looked more comfortable, particularly the full backs Grey and Shaw who were recieved to see the pressure taken off them as the Russians tired.

Rangers started to dominate and most of their good moves were instigated by either Waddell or Johnstone. When Williamson was brought down in the box it was big George Young who stepped up to take the kick this time, and he made no mistake to give Rangers their deserved equaliser.

Many Rangers fans were disappointed at not getting into Ibrox to witness the historic match. But those who were there revelled in a great atmosphere. They were nearly able to come away and say; 'I was there the day Rangers beat the great Moscow Dynamo team in 1945' . . . if only Waddell's penalty had gone in!

Teams: *Rangers:* Dawson, Grey, Shaw, Watkins, Young, Symon, Waddell, Gillick, Smith (Duncanson), Williamson, Johnstone.
Moscow Dynamo: Khomich, Radikorsky, Stankevich, Blinkov, Semichastny, Oreshkin, Archangelski, Kartsev, Beskov, Bobrov (Dementiev), Soloviev.

Scottish Cup Semi-Final, 1948

Rangers 1 *(Thornton)* **Hibernian 0**

The clash between Rangers and Hibernian in the semi-final of the Scottish Cup in 1948 would have been an ideal showpiece for the final itself.

By far the two most outstanding club sides at the time, both were battling for the Championship (which was to go to Hibs by two points), and it was hardly surprising that there was a massive crowd when they met in the Cup. Hampden was crammed solid with 143,570 fans, the biggest crowd in Britain for a match other than for an international or cup final. The size of the crowd showed the pulling power of these two great teams in the years just after the War.

Rangers, complete with their 'Iron Curtain' defence, against the powerful forward line of Hibernian. What a recipe for a great cup-tie!

Played on a glorious Easter Saturday, Rangers went into the match smarting from a 1-2 home defeat by Queen's Park the previous week. They had also found their run to the semi-final something of a struggle. Only a Willie Thornton goal at Stranraer saw them over the first hurdle. And in the quarter-final it was a solitary goal again which beat East Fife. The Hibernian players went into the match with greater confidence and, indeed, they were to have the majority of play. But they could not do what Rangers did . . . and that was score the all-important goal.

The only one of the game came on the half-hour when Thornton broke the deadlock. But after that Rangers struggled to hold on to their lead. It was only sterling work by Young at full-back and Woodburn at centre half that prevented an equaliser by the Edinburgh side. And so Rangers reached their first final since 1936 without conceding a goal.

Teams: *Rangers:* Brown, Young, Shaw, McColl, Woodburn, Cox, Waddell, Gillick, Thornton, Duncanson, Rutherford.
Hibernian: Farm, Govan, Shaw, Kean, Howie, Buchanan, Smith, Combe, Linwood, Cuthbertson, Turnbull.

Scottish Cup Final, 1964

Rangers 3 *(Millar 2, Brand)* **Dundee 1** *(Cameron)*

Two weeks before this final, a large Hampden crowd had seen Scotland beat England 1-0 thanks to an Alan Gilzean goal. Now, two weeks on, another vast crowd was to see Gilzean play his part in a match of fiery excitement and great enthusiasm.

There were many great individuals on the park, all of whom gave outstanding displays.

In front of goal Rangers looked the more dangerous, particularly with Brand and Millar. But it was right-winger Henderson who proved the real match-winner. Dundee's hero was goalkeeper Bert Slater. Time and time again he would fling himself at the feet of the oncoming Rangers forwards.

Despite Jim Baxter being strangely out of touch, Rangers should still have sewn the game up in the first half but Slater thwarted everything they could throw at him.

However, the relentless pressure paid off in the 66th minute. A

Henderson corner was missed by Ryden and up popped Millar to head home. But Dundee responded immediately. When Stuart lobbed a ball downfield, it came off Greig's head and into the path of Cameron who smashed a great shot into the roof of the net from about 15 yards.

Despite conceding the equaliser, Rangers still looked the more likely to score again, particularly when Henderson had the ball. In the last minute he darted to the left side of the field to collect a Baxter free kick, swung the ball into the area and found the head of Millar on the edge of the six-yard box. In went goal number two.

Thirty seconds later, as the Rangers fans were dancing and celebrating on the terraces, Henderson again raced down his wing before passing to Wilson. His shot was saved by Slater but Brand was on hand to put home the rebound. And suddenly, from looking like going into extra-time, Rangers had clinched the cup for the 18th time.

It was Rangers' third consecutive win, and it completed a clean sweep of domestic honours. They had one man to thank for their success – Willie Henderson. Every time he got away from his pursuers he looked capable of changing the game. That is exactly what he did in one of the most dramatic finishes to a Scottish Cup Final.

Teams: *Rangers:* Ritchie, Shearer, Provan, Grieg, McKinnon, Baxter, Henderson, McLean, Millar, Brand, Wilson.
Dundee: Slater, Hamilton, Cox, Seith, Ryden, Stuart, Penman, Cousin, Cameron, Gilzean, Robertson.

League Cup Final, 1970

Rangers 1 *(Johnstone)* **Celtic 0**

This was a dream-come-true for Rangers' 16-year-old Derek Johnstone, the youngest player ever to appear in a British cup final. Rangers had not won a major domestic trophy since beating Celtic to win the Scottish Cup in 1966. In the four-and-a-half years since then they had agonisingly to sit back and watch their arch-rivals take over Scottish football as Celtic won the championship four times, League Cup four times, Scottish Cup twice, and conquer Europe.

The new breed of Rangers fan had only the legend to live on. They desperately wanted success; so did the new breed of players in the side. And this was the chance they had all been waiting for . . . to turn the Rangers legend into present-day reality.

But Rangers faced an uphill task. Celtic were heading for their sixth successive championship and had won the League Cup for the last five seasons. Celtic had won the league meeting six weeks earlier, and to pile on the agony for Rangers, skipper John Greig was out of the team with 'flu.

In Ronnie McKinnon, however, they found an ample replacement for Greig. He was solid and a great inspiration to the youngsters around him.

Celtic started the game casually, and appeared to show little respect for their opponents. That was to prove fatal.

Alfie Conn, Alex MacDonald and Willie Henderson – playing as well as he did in the 1966 Scottish Cup Final against Celtic – all had an outstanding first half for Rangers.

The only goal of a tough but fair game came five minutes before the interval.

Willie Johnston collected a pass from MacDonald and put in a cross which young teenager Johnstone got his head to despite being marked by McNeill and Craig. It was a moment he was to savour for the rest of his life.

Despite being underdogs, Rangers played the better football and many of the 106,000 crowd were left wondering how Celtic were only one down at the interval.

The pattern was the same in the second period, with Rangers having the better of the play. The youngsters held on for a great win and Greig was one of the first men on to the field to congratulate them. How sad it must have been for him to miss this moment of triumph after his role as the backbone of the team during its lean years.

Manager Willie Waddell, who had taken over the previous season, played the win down by saying; 'We've a lot to do before we start celebrating'. He added he would not be happy until Rangers conquered Europe. This win over Celtic was, however, the springboard to that European glory two years later.

Teams: *Rangers:* McCloy, Jardine, Millar, Conn, McKinnon, Jackson, Henderson, MacDonald, Johnstone, Stein, Johnston.
Celtic: Williams, Craig, Quinn, Murdoch, McNeill, Hay, J. Johnstone, Connelly, Wallace, Hood (Lennox), Macari.

European Cup-Winners' Cup, Semi-Final (2nd Leg), 1972

Rangers 2 *(Jardine, Parlane)* **Bayern Munich 0**
(Rangers won 3-1 on aggregate)

Having held Bayern Munich to a 1-1 draw in the first leg, and with the luxury of an away goal, Rangers were ready to settle a score with their German opponents.

Bayern beat Rangers 1-0 in the final of the Cup-Winners' Cup in 1967 and in 1970 knocked the Light Blues out at the first hurdle in the Fairs Cup. But Rangers were aiming for their third final and started the second leg as favourites and full of confidence.

Right from the start it was apparent that Rangers were not going to call upon their away goal to settle the tie and when Jardine scored in the first minute, the 80,000 fans nearly raised the roof of the Ibrox stand.

Johnstone cleverly switched play from the left and McLean touched the ball on to Jardine who hit a first-timer from more than 20 yards. Goalkeeper Sepp Maier just stood and watched the ball enter the net. Four minutes later it was nearly all over when a Stein header beat the 'keeper, but unfortunately it did not beat the crossbar.

After their dream start, Rangers continued to dominate, but not quite with the same fluency. Then, in the 23rd minute, the tie was settled. Mathieson was the instigator of an attack and his cross was desperately cleared for a corner by Koppenhofer. Johnston took the kick which Maier could only push out to Parlane who hammered the ball straight into the net.

For Parlane, making his European debut as stand-in for skipper John Greig, it was the icing on the cake of a brilliant individual performance. He had played only two league games all season but he stepped into the skipper's role in the heart of the defence like a veteran.

Bayern knew they had to attack right from the start after the break if they

were going to get a result. They needed two goals to get back into the match but their best effort came right after the restart. Hoeness, by far the most impressive of the German forwards, broke away and hit a powerful testing shot. McCloy did well to palm the ball on to a post and out for a corner. But that was about the extent of the danger to the Rangers goal. Müller and Hoeness had been contained by Jackson and Johnstone. Consequently, the Bayern attack was virtually non-existent.

The Light Blues took control once more and Jardine, Dave Smith, Alex MacDonald and Tommy McLean, as well as Parlane, deserve singling out for their great individual performances.

Rangers' grit and determination, together with sheer skill, demoralised an otherwise classy Bayern team. The normally elegant Franz Beckenbauer was reduced to scrappy clearances into touch as desperation set in amongst the Bayern defenders.

Having settled the score with Bayern, would it be a case of third time lucky for the Light Blues.

Teams: *Rangers:* McCloy, Jardine, Mathieson, Parlane, Jackson, Smith, McLean, Johnstone, Stein, MacDonald, Johnston.

Colin Stein's header hits the bar in the home leg of the Cup-Winners' Cup semi-final against Bayern Munich in April 1972. Derek Johnstone is second right.

Bayern Munich: Maier, Hansen, Breitner (Rybarczyk), Schwarzenbeck, Beckenbauer, Roth, Schneider, Zobel, Müller, Hoeness, Koppenhofer.

John Greig shoots in the away tie of the 1972 match against Bayern.

European Cup-Winners' Cup Final, 1972

Rangers 3 *(Johnston (2), Stein)* **Moscow Dynamo 2** *(Eschtrekov, Mahovikov)*

In 1945, Moscow Dynamo came to Ibrox and brought with them a new brand of skill and pace. On that day Rangers were very much their equal. Now, 27 years later, Rangers had to go one better if they wanted to lift a European trophy for the first time in their 100-year history, and come out of Celtic's European shadow.

The Italian club Fiorentina in 1961, and Bayern Munich six years later, had thwarted Rangers' hopes of lifting the Cup-Winners' Cup but now, after a great performance against Bayern in the semi-final, Rangers were starting their third final as favourites.

Played under the new floodlights at the 110,000-capacity Nou Camp Stadium in Barcelona, the 25,000 crowd was a mass of blue. An estimated 16,000 fans made the trip from Glasgow, arriving on more than 100 chartered planes, cars and buses. The Moscow Dynamo fans, all 400 of them, came on just three chartered flights!

In the days leading up to the match, Rangers fans had taken over every available hotel room in Barcelona and had a drink in every bar. The Spanish residents were bemused at the thought of men walking round in kilts. It was hard to explain they were not skirts!

The passion of Rangers to win the trophy was matched by the same desire of their Soviet opponents, who were the first Soviet team to reach a European final.

Rangers lined up with an old-fashioned 2–3–5 formation while Dynamo used the 4–3–3 line-up. It was Dynamo who started aggressively and McCloy was soon in action, saving a 25-yard shot from Dolbonosov. Rangers also adopted a shoot-on-sight policy and Pilgui had to dive full-length to save a McLean shot, also from 25 yards.

Midway through the first half the stadium erupted when Rangers took the lead. Johnston went on a run down the right and his centre was met by

Stein who put the ball in from eight yards. Jubilant fans spilled on to the pitch and play was held up for several minutes.

Dynamo pushed forward in search of the equaliser but six minutes before the interval Johnston headed home a Smith cross from the edge of the six-yard box. Dave Smith had been playing magnificently in the heart of the defence. But now he was also playing his part in the attack. Once more, there was a pitch invasion and another delay. The Russians were getting more and more infuriated with the Rangers fans.

Irrespective of what the fans were doing, there was no denying Rangers' superiority on the pitch. Four minutes into the second half and the cup was on its way to Ibrox as Johnston rose to meet a Stein cross for his second, and Rangers' third, goal.

For 50 minutes Rangers monopolised play but on the hour Eschtrekov, who came on as substitute for Jakobik only two minutes earlier, gave some glimmer of hope to the Dynamo fans when he pulled a goal back. But Stern defending by Rangers, particularly Smith, kept future Moscow attacks at bay.

In the closing stages, however, Smith had to kick off the line and Jardine nearly scored an own goal. Three minutes from time Dynamo struck when Mahovikov made it 3-2. Rangers fans' hearts stopped beating for these final few minutes.

But 60 seconds from time the night of glory was marred when thousands of fans spilled on to the pitch thinking the match was over. The players made for the dressing room where John Greig was presented with the cup.

Hardly surprisingly, Moscow Dynamo coach Konstantin Beskov and manager Lev Yashin lodged complaints to UEFA. They appealed for the

Willie Johnston scores his first goal (Rangers' second) in the 1972 European Cup-Winners' Cup final against Moscow Dynamo in Barcelona.

Preceding pages Rangers'
skipper Graham Roberts moves
away from Aberdeen's John
Hewitt in the 1987 Skol Cup
final.

game to be replayed because it was abnormal 'due to the frequent interference of fans'. It was the first time such a request had been put to UEFA after a major final.

Spanish police did not show any restraint in attempting to deal with the final pitch invasion. Many fans were injured and many were arrested.

Just as Rangers had increased their status in Europe with a great win, the club's future in UEFA competitions looked to be in jeopardy. Happily UEFA did not order a replay, but Rangers were banned from all European competitions for two years. This was later reduced to one year on appeal. But, no matter what the punishment, Rangers had, at last, got their hands on a European trophy after 16 years and 83 matches.

1972 European Cup-Winners'
Cup final, Barcelona: Rangers
fans invade the pitch after the
final whistle. The Spanish police
reacted with a mixture of panic
and brutality.

Teams: *Rangers:* McCloy, Jardine, Mathieson, Greig, Johnstone, Smith, McLean, Conn, Stein, MacDonald, Johnston.
Moscow Dynamo: Pilgui, Basalaycev, Dolmatov, Zykov, Dolbonosov (Gerschkovich), Zukov, Baidazhnyi, Jakobik (Eschtrekov), Sabo, Mahovikov, Evriuschkin.

Skol Cup Final, 1986

Rangers 2 *(Durrant, Cooper (pen))* **Celtic 1** *(McClair)*

After just two months into Graeme Souness's first full season in charge at Ibrox, Rangers were a transformed team. New faces had come into the side, but more important, a new spirit was flowing through the club. A trip to Hampden for the Skol Cup final against the arch rivals was ample proof of the success of Souness's tactics.

This was the 10th League Cup final involving the two giants of Scottish football. The scoreline read 5-4 to Rangers going into the match, but Celtic stood at the top of the Premier Division with Rangers in third place.

Skol Cup final 1986: Ian Durrant (left) turns in triumph after scoring Rangers' first goal; Terry Butcher is at extreme right, Ted McMinn is at bottom. Celtic players: Pat Bonner (1), Derek White (5), Murdo Macleod (10).

Sadly, many top games early in the season had been influenced by poor refereeing and this potentially great game went the same way. It has to be said that Rutherglen referee David Syme lost control of the match.

Souness was absent from the Rangers line-up through injury and the game, as a spectacle, did not come to life until Durrant put Rangers ahead in the 62nd minute with a 12-yard shot. That sparked Celtic and they piled on sustained pressure which was rewarded when McClair netted a glorious equaliser a couple of minutes later.

From that point Celtic looked the likely winners but, with no more goals apparent, extra-time looked likely. But then, seven minutes from time, the game was turned into a farce!

Celtic's Roy Aitken and Terry Butcher challenged for the ball from a Ferguson free kick and as the two big men went up referee Syme awarded a penalty to Rangers. The fans and players could not believe it. Mo Johnston was sent off for an off-the-ball incident, and 10 players were cautioned. The Celtic players crowded round the referee in protest and he showed the red card to Shepherd. For some inexplicable reason he did not go off and was allowed to carry on playing.

It was only after Celtic manager David Hay came on to the field to restore order that the game continued. Hay was so incensed with the standard of refereeing, not only in this match, but in other top Scottish matches, that he stormed: 'If it was anything to do with me I would make an application to join the English League.'

Davie Cooper, who missed the early part of the season through

Preceding pages *Robert Fleck
(8) scores Rangers' third goal to
equalise with three minutes
remaining in the 1987 Skol Cup
final against Aberdeen.*

suspension, stepped up to score from the spot kick. The rest of the match
fizzled out as Rangers won their 14th League Cup trophy. It was a game that
will be remembered not for its quality of football, but for the way it was
handled by the official in charge.

Teams: *Rangers:* Woods, Nicholl, Munro, Fraser (McFarlane), Dawson,
Butcher, Ferguson, McMinn, McCoist (Fleck), Durrant, Cooper.
Celtic: Bonner, Grant, MacLeod, Aitken, Whyte, McGhee (Archdeacon),
McClair, McStay, Johnston, Shepherd, McInally.

Skol Cup Final, 1987

Rangers 3 *(Cooper, Durrant, Fleck)* **Aberdeen 3** *(Bett (pen), Hewitt,
Falconer)*
(Rangers won 5-3 on penalties)

In contrast to the previous year's final, this game was a treat for the 71,893
fans at Hampden.

Even the most ardent of Rangers fans would agree that to conclude such a
great match with a penalty shoot-out was inappropriate and it was
unfortunate there had to be a loser.

The match could have gone either way as the 120 minutes play produced
end-to-end football and countless goalmouth incidents. Rangers twice came
from behind and Aberdeen had also to pull back after Rangers went 2-1 up.

The scoring feast started in the eighth minute when Rangers 'keeper
Walker playing his first senior game for 14 months, and only in the team
because of Chris Woods' suspension, brought down Falconer, which allowed
Bett to score from the penalty spot.

With the majority of the large crowd Rangers fans, they spurred their
team on and in the 22nd minute Cooper equalised with a fierce free kick.
Five minutes before the interval, the Light Blues took the lead. Durrant, who
had an outstanding game, played a great one-two with fellow Scottish
international Ally McCoist before driving past the despairing Leighton.

Rangers then dominated the game until the 72nd minute when a Joe
Miller cross was only half cleared and Hewitt followed up to drive home the
equaliser.

Extra-time was imminent, but nine minutes from normal time Falconer
headed home Bett's cross and suddenly it was Aberdeen who thought they
were going to get their hands on the trophy. But Rangers threw every man
forward in an effort to get a second equaliser. They did not have to wait
long.

After showing his superiority in the air, Durrant won a ball that fell for
Fleck, who had no trouble scoring from close range.

With so many tired legs, the extra 30-minute period was expected to
bring the game to a sedate close. Rangers had a great chance when Durrant
put McCoist through, but the striker missed. Then it was Aberdeen's turn
but Walker brought off a good save from Weir. But there were to be no more
goals, so the penalty shoot-out was called upon for the first time in a major
final. Aberdeen's Peter Nicholas hit the top of the crossbar with the second
of his team's five spot kicks. All Rangers had to do was convert all five to win
the cup. And that is what they did. Furthermore, it was appropriate that the
match-winning fifth and final kick should be converted by the outstanding
Durrant.

Rangers took their tally of League Cup wins to 15 and, as they had won the new Skol Cup for a third time, were allowed to keep the trophy. It was just unfortunate there was not another trophy to give Aberdeen because they certainly played their part in making it a great match.

Robert Fleck (left) battles with Dons' skipper Willie Miller in the 1987 Skol Cup final.

Teams: *Rangers:* Walker, Nicholl, Munro, Roberts, Ferguson (Francis), Gough, McGregor (Cohen), Fleck, McCoist, Durrant, Cooper.
Aberdeen: Leighton, McKimmie, Connor, Simpson (Weir), McLeish, W. Miller, Hewitt, Bett, J. Miller, Nicholas, Falconer.

121

Index

Acknowledgements

The publishers would like to thank the following for their kind permission to reproduce the illustrations in this book:

Action Plus Photographic 46–7, 112

Colorsport Endpapers 6–7, 10–11, 34–5, 36, 37, 48, 49, 52, 53, 55, 59, 60, 61, 74, 80, 85, 86–7, 88, 98, 102–3, 113, 118–9

Glasgow Herald & Evening Times 12–13, 17, 18, 19, 20, 21, 22, 23, 25, 26, 28–9, 30, 31, 33, 75, 76, 92, 93, 96, 99, 100, 101, 105, 107

The Scotsman 41, 44, 50, 70–1, 97, 111

Sporting Pictures (UK) Ltd 67

Bob Thomas Sports Photography 38–9, 42–3, 69, 82–3, 90–1, 94–5, 114–5